NO SECOND CHANCES

A FEMINIST HISTORY SOCIETY BOOK

NO SECOND CHANCES

WOMEN AND POLITICAL POWER IN CANADA

KATE GRAHAM

Second Story Press

Library and Archives Canada Cataloguing in Publication

Title: No second chances : women and political power in Canada / Kate Graham.
Names: Graham, Kate, 1984- author.
Series: Feminist history society series.
Description: Series statement: A feminist history society book | Includes bibliographical
   references and index.
Identifiers: Canadiana (print) 20210297735 | Canadiana (ebook) 20210297808 | ISBN
   9781772602180 (softcover) | ISBN 9781772602197 (EPUB)
Subjects: LCSH: Women politicians—Canada—Biography. | LCSH: Politicians—
   Canada—Biography. | LCSH: Women legislators—Canada—Biography. | LCSH:
   Legislators—Canada—Biography. | LCSH: Women—Political activity—Canada. |
   LCSH: Political leadership—Canada. | LCGFT: Biographies.
Classification: LCC FC26.P6 G73 2022 | DDC 324.2092/52—dc23

www.FeministHistories.ca

Cover by Ingrid Paulson

Edited by Andrea Knight

Printed and bound in Canada

*Second Story Press gratefully acknowledges the support of the Ontario Arts Council and
the Canada Council for the Arts for our publishing program. We acknowledge the financial
support of the Government of Canada through the Canada Book Fund.*

Published by
Second Story Press
20 Maud Street, Suite 401
Toronto, ON M5V 2M5
www.secondstorypress.ca

For Deb Matthews.
Thanks for asking.

CONTENTS

NO
SEC✗ND
CHANCES

PREFACE

In 2018, I did something that not enough women in Canada have done: I ran for office. I was working as a public servant at the time, and when I shared my decision with family, friends, and colleagues, the feedback was less than encouraging:

"But don't you want to have kids?"

"Why would you quit your six-figure job on a chance? What about your pension?"

"Are you sure you want to put yourself through that?"

The months that followed proved to be an education like no other. I spent hours each day knocking on doors. I stood on tens of thousands of doorsteps and listened to what people had to say. I was running for the Ontario Liberal Party led by Kathleen Wynne—the only female premier in Ontario's history and the first openly gay premier in Canada. She had led the party to victory in 2014 and was seeking a second mandate.

It was an angry election. To put it bluntly, Premier Wynne was hated. Front lawns sported "Unplug Wynne" signs in reference to divisive hydro issues. Social media ads frequently flashed unflattering photos of the premier's face with a thick line through it. According to the polls, more than 70 per cent of Ontarians disapproved of the premier and the numbers only grew worse as the campaign waged on. When the premier visited our riding for campaign events, we had protesters at the campaign office.

On election night, the party suffered the worst defeat in its history, falling from a majority government to losing official party status. Almost all the party's caucus and every new candidate lost, including me.

Every election has its policy disputes and that was certainly true in Ontario in 2018, but this election felt particularly personal. During the campaign I had listened to thousands of people talk about the premier. I had the same conversation over and over again.

"You seem fine, but I can't support your leader. She has to go."

I always replied calmly, asking the same question: "What is it about the premier that you don't like?"

This would be met with a long pause and then, too often, one of the following replies:

"It's the sound of her voice. I just can't stand it."

"It's her face." (Yes, people really did say this.)

"I just *really* can't stand her."

Long after the election ended, I could not erase these conversations from my mind. I began reading about the defeats of other female premiers in Canada. I was surprised to find similar media stories from other provinces about the unpopular, seemingly unlikable women who led them. The shared "glass cliff" experience—a term from the business world about female CEOs rising to the top job only when the company was facing decline—was all too common. I calculated the average tenure for premiers, only to find that it is significantly shorter for women. And most concerningly, when female premiers run for re-election, they lose. Canadians have never re-elected a female first minister.[1]

I needed to learn more. With the support of Canada 2020, an Ottawa-based policy think tank, I travelled across Canada to meet with the women who have led our provinces, territories, and country. We spent hours in their kitchens, living rooms, and front

....

[1] Depending on how this is defined, the one exception to this pattern is Christy Clark, former premier of British Columbia. In the first general election after Clark became party leader, the party formed the government, but Clark lost her own seat. She continued as leader and premier and later won a seat in a by-election. In her second general election, Clark's party won the most seats but came one seat short of forming government, and other parties formed a coalition government. Clark resigned shortly afterward.

porches talking about the rise and fall of their political careers. I asked them to help me understand why we don't see female political leaders succeeding in Canada to the same extent as men. These conversations formed the basis of a podcast project called *No Second Chances*. More than 75,000 Canadians have listened to the podcast, and we heard from many people (mostly women) who found the stories of Canada's female leaders to be inspiring and motivating.

One of the limitations of podcasting is that the interviews are cut into short clips, so listeners don't have the opportunity to hear the speakers in long form. This book is intended to address this deficiency. It presents the perspectives of the first ministers in long form.[2] It captures an important part of Canadian history and preserves the perspectives of the small group of trailblazing women who have risen to Canada's peak political posts. Importantly, these interviews were conducted in 2019, a moment in time when every single first minister in Canada was a man, a sorry statement about the intersection of gender and political leadership in our country. This book captures a contemporary reflection on how and why this happened, and what can be done to make greater progress toward gender equity in political leadership in the future.

My hope is that a Canadian picking up this book fifty or a hundred years in the future will find its contents foreign and peculiar. The experiences of women in Canada's most senior political roles shed much light on the reasons why there have been so few of them in the first place.

I hope it will also seem unusual that this book includes only the perspectives of Indigenous and white women. To date, a Black

....

[2] As of the writing of this book, there had been thirteen female first ministers in Canada to date. This book features twelve of them: ten who were interviewed for the *No Second Chances* podcast by author Kate Graham; Pauline Marois, who at her request was interviewed by a Francophone journalist, Noémi Mercier from Radio-Canada, for a French episode of the podcast; and, Caroline Cochrane, who was elected after the *No Second Chances* podcast project was complete, so a subsequent interview was completed with Kate Graham in August 2021. Unfortunately, Rita Johnston from British Columbia, the first female premier in Canada, was not able to be interviewed due to her health. The podcast form of most of these discussions is available at NoSecondChances.ca. The fourteenth female first minister, Heather Stefanson, took office as premier of Manitoba in October 2021, after the writing of this book.

or racialized woman has never been elected as a first minister in Canada. In fact, many equity-seeking groups have never been represented in our top elected offices. It is only Canada's territories that have elected Indigenous women as their premiers.

This must change.

The lack of diversity within our most senior parliamentary levels is one of the reasons that, as a country, we have not advanced further on many of the most significant challenges we face.

The research is clear. Until we see more women—and a greater diversity of women—in our highest political offices, we will not be able to address the deep inequalities that exist in our country. It is that simple. Having a greater number and diversity of women in the most senior leadership roles will lead to decisions being made that benefit more people. Similarly, the election of women to those roles is a marker, or a product, of the extent to which our society has evolved into one in which opportunities are truly equal. A lack of diversity in our top political roles is a sign of a much more concerning imbalance and injustice in the society our politicians govern. It's like the seemingly benign physical symptoms that signal a much more serious disease underneath.

This book has been written to share the insightful, sometimes funny, and often inspirational perspectives of the women who have examined our political institutions and culture from the highest vantage point. It is not an evaluation or an expression of these women's political agendas or policy accomplishments. They span partisan stripes across jurisdictions and over a long period of time. It is likely that they would even disagree with one another on many important policy matters. Instead, this book shares without judgment the firsthand perspectives of a small but important group of Canadian leaders who don't fit the mould of most of our nation's most senior political leaders. They have ideological differences, but they share the experience of breaking through barriers that have kept out others like them for so long. Ultimately, they are an important part of the broader project to motivate Canadians to seek out, support, and vote for a greater diversity of political leaders in the future.

If, like me, you feel indebted to the women featured in the pages that follow, there is nothing greater you can do.

INTRODUCTION

When you are not prototypical—when you are not like others who have done the job—it becomes very difficult for people to overcome their visceral sense that something is not quite right. So you never get the benefit of the doubt because people need to reconcile that sense of discomfort they have that you're not someone who looks and sounds like they are used to. The only way to change this is to change the landscape from which people get their sense of how the world works[.... W]hen you are the first in something—whether you're the first woman or first member of your ethnic group or the first of any group that's not prototypical—well, there are a few human sacrifices. When we talk about why there aren't so many second chances, it's because it takes a long time to reprogram those expectations to make people look at you and say, that's what the prime minister looks like or that's what a premier looks like.

These words were spoken by Kim Campbell, the nineteenth prime minister of Canada, in Ottawa on June 19, 2019, at the first ever gathering of Canada's female first ministers. The event celebrated the conclusion of Canada 2020's *No Second Chances* project. This project examined the experiences of women who served in Canada's most senior political roles as first ministers—prime minister or premier—as a window into the dynamics of Canadian politics for women in leadership. The event occurred shortly after Rachel Notley's loss as premier of Alberta, creating yet another moment in Canadian history with exactly zero women around the first ministers' table.

All of the women participated in interviews about their experiences, most of them in their homes. The collective story of their political rise and fall was shared in the *No Second Chances* podcast, augmented with videos and other smaller events along the way. This culminating gathering in Ottawa was historic—surprisingly, many of the women had never met each other. Just before the main event, the women gathered over lunch and used this time to collectively pen an Open Letter to Canadians about what needs to change to see more women in senior elected offices in Canada. It was released later that same day and is included in the Appendix to this volume.

When Campbell took the stage for the closing keynote address, she spoke about how difficult it was to watch Hillary Clinton's two failed attempts to break through the highest political glass ceiling in the world: first to become the Democratic presidential candidate in 2008, losing to Barack Obama, and then to become president as the Democratic candidate against Donald Trump in 2016. Campbell remarked how people often pointed to Clinton as a "flawed candidate" to rationalize or explain these losses:

> We try to rewrite these elections to justify all the mean things we said about her and the things we said about her emails and the double standards we applied to her. We try to justify this by describing her as a "flawed candidate." Well, you know what? We are all flawed candidates. No one is perfect and we all step in it and we all make mistakes. Equality for women will come when we are forgiven at the same rate that men are.

CANADA'S FIRST MINISTERS

As of the writing of this book, a total of 315 people have served in Canada's top political post as a first minister.[3] And, to use Campbell's words, we most definitely have "a type."

- MALE. A man has led Canada for 99.8 per cent of the days since Confederation, and men have led our provinces and territories for 97.2 per cent of the days those jurisdictions have collectively been a part of Canada. We have had thirty first ministers named John, and only thirteen women.[4]

- WHITE. Among our top political leaders since Confederation, 94 per cent have been white. The second-largest group represented is Indigenous, almost all of them serving as premiers of the Northwest Territories and Nunavut.

- OLDER. The average age of our first ministers (upon attaining that office) is 61.5 years old, much older than the average Canadian. For many, reaching a first minister position marks the final major post of their career. The average age of a newly elected first minister has increased over time—it was just forty-eight in the 1800s—although there has been a decrease in the past two decades. Importantly, the average age for female first ministers is almost a decade younger (52.1) than it is for male first ministers.

- CHRISTIAN. To date, very few leaders in Canada, of any gender, have been members of faith communities outside of Christianity.

....

[3] This definition of "top political role" is based on Canada's constitutional arrangements, which unfortunately did not appropriately recognize Indigenous communities or municipalities as governments within Canada. The data in this section also assumes a "start date" of 1867, at the time of Confederation, although of course there were many leaders—men and women—serving before this time in what later became Canada.

[4] The fourteenth, Premier Heather Stefanson of Manitoba, was sworn into office shortly after this book was completed.

- HETEROSEXUAL. It is only very recently that any first ministers have openly identified as being lesbian or gay, such as Ontario's Kathleen Wynne or Prince Edward Island's Wade MacLauchlan. It is hoped that greater diversity including sexual orientation and gender expression of our leaders is yet to come, including a first minister who identifies as trans or nonbinary.

- AFFLUENT, EDUCATED, AND ESTABLISHED. At least 144 of the 315 (45 per cent) of those who have served as a first ministers were trained as lawyers before entering politics. If we add a background in business to the mix, then the number becomes more than 66 per cent. At least ninety-six of our first ministers have had a family member who is also in politics, including sixty-eight with a political father.

In other words, Canada's top political leaders reflect *privilege*. They represent groups that have benefitted from the many advantages afforded to them when it comes to securing our top political roles. Even the few who break this mould, including the women featured in this book, are almost all white women. People who don't fit this profile too often face insurmountable obstacles in seeking the most senior political offices. Over the arc of our history, our political system has proven effective in keeping some groups in and keeping other groups out.

HIGH CEILINGS AND GLASS CLIFFS

Why haven't more women risen to the top in Canada? In the early decades of Canadian political leadership, the answer was painfully simple. Women did not even have the right to vote until well into the 1900s. Some women in Manitoba (not including First Nations and Inuit women) were the first to gain the vote in 1916, but the franchise wasn't extended to women across Canada until decades later. Women in Québec were not allowed to vote until 1940. The right to vote and seek elected office led to a steady progression of important firsts: women elected as members across levels of government; women appointed to cabinet positions; women elected as party leaders; and, finally, women leading governments. The pathways to these roles varied. Canada's first female first minister, Rita Johnston, became premier of British Columbia in April 1991; she won the leadership race just as her party was falling into political oblivion, never to form government again. The second female first minister, Nellie Cournoyea, was appointed by her elected colleagues through the territory's consensus model and became premier of the Northwest Territories in November 1991. The first woman to become a first minister in Canada by leading her party through a general election was Catherine Callbeck in Prince Edward Island in 1993. It is only in the past three decades that we have seen women serving as Canadian first ministers at all.

Canada's colonial and patriarchal institutional foundations were an impenetrable barrier for women seeking to hold political leadership roles during our first 124 years as a nation, but women have now been voting for more than a century and have held nearly every significant political leadership role in the country. However, as gains have been made toward gender equality in many sectors and parts of society, why haven't we made more progress in political leadership? Why do almost all our top political leaders *still* reflect the same characteristics?

Part of the answer is found in the broader problem that women remain underrepresented throughout Canadian politics. The well-documented reasons for this chronic and persistent underrepresentation include multiple external factors built into our political institutions—literature identifies "barriers" as parts of the political process that are more difficult for women—as well as into our political culture (for example, sexism in the media), and into our society (such as gender inequality that results in higher rates of poverty for women along with disproportionate family responsibilities). In addition to these external factors, there are a number of internal factors—most of them stemming from socialization within a patriarchal culture—that prevent women from seeking and holding elected office. Studies comparing men and women with similar resumes on how qualified they feel to hold elected office have repeatedly found significant disparities between the two—sometimes called the "confidence gap"—and more frequent instances of "imposter syndrome" among women seeking or holding elected positions. Together, this

constellation of external and internal factors has produced a stub-
bornly low number of women in elected office across governments in
Canada, which in turn creates a "pipeline" problem by reducing the
pool of women well-positioned for promotion to leadership roles.
This is sometimes described as "the higher, the fewer" phenomenon.

When women do attain political leadership roles, they face
an added layer of challenges. Political scientist Sylvia Bashevkin
describes "the discomfort equation" in Canada, a form of subconscious bias in which Canadians experience a sense of dissonance
when they see women and power together. She argues that
Canadians have acquired a "highly virulent strain" of this bias that
associates female political leaders with electoral failures. Seeing
Canada's few female political leaders often rise to general visibility
in high-profile moments of their party's political decline—take, for
example, Kim Campbell or Rita Johnston—has shaped our overall
perception of women political leaders so that many Canadians now
associate them with defeat and even humiliation. This hinders the
efforts to see more women in political leadership on multiple levels:
it may create a perception or bias among voters that disadvantages
female would-be leaders; it may disincentivize political parties and
the people engaged in recruiting for them from seeking out and supporting women for senior political roles; and, if the risk of failure
is seen to be high, it may discourage women from taking on such
high-profile endeavours in the first place.

Even if Canadians' discomfort at seeing women in power is
mostly experienced in subtle or unconscious ways, we may have fundamentally misunderstood the dynamics at play in these moments
of defeat. The concept of the "glass cliff" originated in business and
follows the argument that women only rise to positions of power
at times when the company is already falling into decline. In other
words, the rise of women occurs only in times where the odds of
success are low, making their ability to succeed in those roles even
more challenging, if not impossible. Some of the interviews that
follow suggest this dynamic is at play in Canadian politics. Former
British Columbia Premier Christy Clark, for example, pointedly
described her decision to run for leader in this way: "there was no
reason to think we would win the next election [so] nobody good
wanted to do it." Women who become leaders toward the end of a

government's mandate or in the wake of a leader with failing popularity take on an even greater challenge. If they fail in this effort, as the experience of Kim Campbell shows, we compound the challenge of female leaders by assigning the electoral outcome to gender.

In sum, there are multiple complex and intersecting reasons why Canada's top political leaders continue to reflect a prototype of older, white, affluent, straight, able-bodied men. Female leaders face all the barriers that have long kept women from achieving parity in political participation, and they face added barriers when rising to positions of leadership because of the ways they are perceived as leaders and the political dynamics in which they rise.

But what happens when women do reach the top? What can we learn about Canadian politics and political culture by examining the rise and fall of the few women who have made it to our most senior political posts?

NO SECOND CHANCES

The re-election of incumbents is common in Canada. This is a well-established feature of Canadian politics across all levels of government. Mayoral elections that include an incumbent mayor generally see a significantly lower voter turnout—often because the stakes are not seen to be particularly high. For members of provincial, territorial, or federal parliaments, incumbency brings many advantages at election time, such as more resources, higher name recognition, and the benefit of a four-year runway to build a relationship with voters. In Canada and within provinces, a very small number of dominant political parties generally hold or swap power between them, making it extremely difficult for new political parties to break through.

Canadians re-elect incumbents all the time—*except* when it comes to female first ministers. In fact, as of 2021, Canadians have never re-elected a female first minister.

Some well-informed readers may question this statement. Kathleen Wynne, for example, became premier of Ontario when she won a leadership race while her party was in government. She then led her party to a stunning general electoral victory in 2014. Doesn't that count? Wynne and Alberta's Rachel Notley led their parties to electoral victory exactly once. When Wynne ran as premier in a second general election, her party dropped to its lowest seat count in history and lost official party status. British Columbia's Christy Clark has come the closest to defying the trend. Clark led her party to victory in the 2013 general election but lost her own seat. She ran in a by-election shortly after and continued to lead the party through to the 2017 general election, where once again her party won the most seats. However, they came one seat short of forming government, and a coalition was promptly formed by two other parties. Clark resigned shortly afterward.

This is the "no second chances" problem in Canada: when female first ministers run for re-election, they lose.

Canada's 302 male first ministers have served for an average of 1,874 days, roughly five years. This means that, on average, their service spans two terms. For the thirteen female first ministers, this average is 1,142 days, or about three years, generally less than one term. This is roughly 60 per cent of the tenure of male first ministers. Even when the political tenure of female first ministers is considered only among first ministers who have served in the past three decades—since 1991, when the first female first ministers rose to power, a period in which political tenures on average have been shorter for all first ministers—there is still a significant gap, with female first ministers serving about 65 per cent of the average tenure of men.

How are we to account for the imbalance? At the outset of the *No Second Chances* project, we shared a few promotional videos highlighting this disparity. We received some chirps online, such as "it's because all of them were terrible leaders!" or "they were all corrupt!" These were too often accompanied with some less repeatable content. The comments laid bare our tendency to lay the blame for electoral fortunes with the women themselves. Sound familiar, "flawed candidates" Kim Campbell and Hillary Clinton?

That project, and this book, are premised on a rather different starting assumption. If we don't see many women reach or hold our top political roles, perhaps we ought to focus less on finding flaws among the few who rise to the top and instead ask ourselves what this says about us as Canadians. Perhaps what we need is a good, hard look in the mirror.

The pages to follow feature the words of most of the very small group of women who have experienced the highs and lows of Canadian politics. They have seen the dynamics at play from the highest vantage point and know all too well where the fault lines lie for women in senior political leadership roles. The content has been edited for brevity and readability, but careful attention was paid to keeping the expression and ideas intact.

To any who question whether this group's electoral fortunes are a product of some perceived deficiency on their part, I challenge you to read particularly carefully. What you will find is a group of unusually bright, driven, capable, and insightful leaders. Their political careers span three decades and political stripes; collectively they provide a coast-to-coast-to-coast perspective on politics and leadership in Canada. Some of what they have experienced reflects far less about them as leaders and far more about us as Canadians and our political systems.

And you may find yourself questioning whether "no second chances" is about the losses faced by our female leaders or the loss we face as a country when we don't see women succeed.

"I'd really like people to feel they can stand on my shoulders in the sense that I stood on the shoulders of the people who went before." Kim Campbell is Canada's first, and so far only, woman prime minister.

KIM CAMPBELL

PRIME MINISTER OF CANADA
(1993)

In the 154 years since Confederation, Canada has been led by a female prime minister for just 132 days. On June 25, 1993, Kim Campbell made history when she became Canada's first female prime minister.

Today, she still stands alone as the one and only.

Avril Phaedra Douglas Campbell was born in Port Alberni, British Columbia in 1947. When their parents' marriage began to fall apart, she and her sister were sent to boarding school. A call from her father when she was twelve brought the difficult news that her mother had left. The girls didn't see their mother again for another ten years. For Avril, it was a defining moment. She set out to choose her own path forward and, as a teenager, decided to change her name to Kim. As a preteen, Campbell was a co-host on CBC's *Junior Television Club*. She was on the student council at nearly every stage in her educational career and became the first female president of the University of British Columbia's freshman class. She was elected as a trustee for the Vancouver School Board in 1980 while attending law school and became the board chair just two years later.

In 1983, Kim Campbell ran as a Social Credit candidate in Vancouver Centre for a seat in the British Columbia legislative assembly. She lost. Three years later, she ran for the leadership of the Social Credit Party. Again, she lost—placing last, garnering only fourteen delegate votes—but she gave a speech at the convention that brought the room to its feet and put Campbell on the map as a rising political star. Soon after, in 1988, she ran federally and was elected as the member of Parliament for Vancouver Centre. She was quickly appointed to Cabinet, first as minister of state for Indian affairs and northern development. In 1990, she became Canada's first female minister of justice and attorney general. Campbell had many policy accomplishments in this role, such as introducing significant gun control measures in the wake of the 1989 École Polytechnique massacre in Montréal. She also established changes to the criminal code to protect women, including updating the definition of consent and introducing the Rape Shield Law that prevented an individual's sexual past from being used during a trial. In 1993, Prime Minister Brian Mulroney and the federal Progressive Conservatives were facing declining public support with an election looming. Mulroney resigned, triggering a leadership race for a party in less-than-ideal circumstances. Campbell ran for the leadership and this time she won. In June 1993, Campbell was elected as party leader, becoming the first female prime minister of Canada. She served in this role for 132 days, the third-shortest term for a Canadian prime minister, leading the Progressive Conservative party through what would become the most devastating loss in the party's history. Campbell even lost her own seat.

Although this wasn't the end of public life for Campbell— among other academic and leadership posts, she went on to serve as Canada's consul general in Los Angeles and chair of the Council of Women World Leaders—it was a harsh ending for Canada's first female prime minister. Not only have Canadians experienced a woman being in our most senior political role for just 132 days of our history as a nation, but we have also seen a woman lead only while her party is facing certain defeat.

I met Kim Campbell in a hotel lobby in Ottawa, where she had been invited to give a keynote address. Most of the *No Second Chances* interviews occurred in the homes of the first ministers, but as Campbell was travelling, we had rented a space in Ottawa that was all set up for audio and video recording. I met Campbell at the hotel where she was staying so we could travel over to the makeshift studio together.

Not minutes after the elevator beeped open, the sense of a celebrity in the room was palpable. People turned to stare. A few asked, "Are you...?" to which Campbell smiled and nodded. As soon as we were on our own, she became far more candid. I got to enjoy her quick wit and direct way of speaking. Between her hotel and the rental studio, we covered a wide array of topics: her take on the current federal government, climate change, elephants in Africa (a passion for her), and dating while in politics. By the time we sat down for the interview, my nerves over interviewing a former prime minister were all but a memory. Campbell was insightful and compelling, and somehow able to describe even the most difficult parts of her story with the perspective (and sometimes even humour) that comes with the passage of time.

Months later, we convened again in Ottawa for the closing event of the *No Second Chances* project—a historic gathering of Canada's female first ministers where Campbell gave the keynote address. At the time, I was teaching a summer course on women and politics, and Huron University College kindly provided support for the twelve students in the class to attend the event in Ottawa with me. After the event concluded, the students and I went out for dinner, and Kim Campbell joined us. I watched her sit among a group of eager young university students, connecting with them with that same authenticity I had felt moments into our first meeting. One of my students bravely debated Campbell on the merits of mandatory voting, having just submitted a paper on the topic. Campbell gave her a run for her money. When dinner concluded, Campbell left for the night and for a moment my students sat at the restaurant table looking at each other incredulously. "Can you believe that just happened?!"

I started each interview the same way: asking each woman to start at the beginning and share a bit about her childhood and the early influences that led her into politics. Each one had a different story, some with clear connections between their origin story and the political journey that followed. Indeed, to interview Kim Campbell is both an honour and a reminder of the fortitude required to become a one and only.

KIM CAMPBELL: My childhood recedes ever more into the distance as I get older. I realize that as a baby boomer I'm of a particular species. I was born after World War II and both my parents had been in uniform. My mother horrified her mother by joining the navy. She was a wireless operator who tracked the transmissions of German U-boats in the North Atlantic and Gulf of St. Lawrence. I grew up knowing World War II was a big deal. It was everywhere. It was such an enormous event in world history that [there were lots of] books trying to understand how it happened and how to prevent it again and, of course, the construction of all the postwar institutions designed to prevent such a thing from happening again. It was very, very clear in my life. The fact that both my parents had participated, had been part of it—I grew up with a sense of awareness of a world outside my own life, and that there were important things that went on, like global politics.... But I didn't know much about politics in the sense that neither of my parents was particularly political. They voted. They were good citizens. But I didn't have anybody in my family who was a politician. I was much more interested in international issues. When I was a teenager, I wanted to be the first woman secretary general of the UN. I wanted to stop World War III. My mother raised my sister and me to believe that girls could do anything, but to understand that it wasn't a universally accepted proposition. And she raised us to know a lot of interesting stories about women who'd done interesting things. Charlotte Whitton, who was the first woman mayor of Ottawa, had a famous saying that "a woman had to be twice as good as a man in order to be thought half as good, but fortunately that's easy." My mother tried to encourage my sister and me to believe that girls could do things and not to be afraid, to be ambitious and curious....

When I was twelve, my mother had put my sister and me in boarding school in Victoria and my mother left my father. I wound up not seeing her for ten years. So, I had this interesting mix of an upbringing. On the one hand, [I spent] the first twelve years of my life with a mother who was really very supportive of the aspirations of her girls, and really taught my sister and me to love to read, to be curious, to love language, and all that kind of thing. And then to be kind of a freak, to be a teenage girl without a mother. There's a woman named Hope Edelman who wrote a book called *Motherless Daughters*. She talks about how her mother died when she was seventeen. Her mother had cancer and I remember thinking, well, that's a lot more respectable than having your mother run off and you don't know where she is....

[Edelman] says that girls who grow up without mothers tend to be very independent and self-reliant and resistant of gender stereotypes. I certainly was that kind of person, but I think I learned that from my mother. I had already been raised by her to be independent and curious. Whatever we were interested in doing, she would teach us—and there was no question that she wouldn't answer. I remember when I was about five, talking to kids at the end of the street and saying in passing, "Well, you know, little girls come from inside their mothers." The boy said, "Well, I suppose that little boys come from inside their father." I looked at him like he was a total lunatic: you don't know where babies come from? That was one of the first times I realized that not everybody was learning the same things that we were....

I [also] had a sense of being willing to take responsibility for things. When I was in Grade 5, our school was doing a sports day celebrating the centenary of the Union of Vancouver Island and the mainland of British Columbia into one province in 1858. And for our class we were supposed to do something with the 1920s. And I said, "Oh, we should dance the Charleston!" I didn't know how but I had a friend who went to dance school. [So] I organized some girls and I got Sandy to teach us, and we did a little routine. We all borrowed costumes and we were a total hit. I organized it because I just thought we should do it. Years later, in law school, I wound up writing and directing the *Law Revue* because the guy who'd done it for the first two years was tired of it. So I said, "Well, okay, I'll do it." There's a part of me that feels a sense of responsibility. And not just for song and dance, but also...I guess I felt I never could lead a totally self-regarding life. That I had some obligation to the world beyond my own life. It was thinking about how we live in the world and how we manage our lives together as citizens. And it was only later, in my twenties, that I began to think maybe politics might be a way of doing this....

I was teaching at UBC, and I had a young student, Andy Stark, who's now a senior professor at the University of Toronto. He was president of the Young Progressive Conservatives, and he gave me some of Bob Stanfield's speeches. They were quite good. I said to him, "I've thought of going into politics, but I am not involved with a party." He said, "If you want to go into politics, don't get involved in a party. Become a star." What he meant was become somebody that a party will want to be their candidate....

In a sense, I did that by going into municipal politics. My first husband had served on the school board. He was very well known. He was a famous math professor and a lively bon vivant. When he wanted to run for city council, his colleagues came to me and said, "Would you think of running for the school board?" I didn't want to use my married name because my married name was Divinsky, and Campbell is my maiden name. I've always used it. And I said, "I don't use my married name professionally." And they all went, "Oh...," because they thought if I used my married name, for sure I'd get elected because my husband had been so famous. And I thought that was dishonest. Anyway, to make a long story short; he ran for city council, I ran for school board. We both got elected but I got more votes than he did. That was my first foray into elected politics, in 1980. It was the same year that I started law school. I was trained as a Soviet specialist in political science. I won't even go into the long story about the sexism around why I didn't have a job—which wasn't at UBC, it was another place. I wasn't going to get a [job]...and I had begun to lose my taste for having a career in academia. I loved what I had done in graduate work at the London School of Economics, I [had even] spent three months in the Soviet Union. But I realized that I needed to retrain to do something else. And going to law school wasn't because I necessarily wanted to be a lawyer but because I thought law was a good discipline for doing other things. I've always loved being a lawyer. I think the rule of law is one of the most amazing things that human societies have created. It is precious and it's the most fundamental value of a democracy. I practiced briefly but then went to work [in politics].... I'd run provincially [before] I went to work in the premier's office in British Columbia. And I realized I wasn't cut out to be a political staffer. But it's sort of a long story.

KATE GRAHAM: Let's hear the long story.

KIM CAMPBELL: Well, after the school board and in my third year of law school, I was asked by one of the premier's advisors if I'd be willing to run in the provincial election in Vancouver Centre. It was an NDP [New Democratic Party] riding and it was unlikely we were going to be able to win it, but they thought if they had high-profile candidates it would tie them down. I said, "Sure, as long as it's not when I'm writing my law school exams." And he looked sort of pale because he couldn't tell me when it was going to be…and sure enough I wrote my finals while I was a candidate for the legislature. I am happy to say that I graduated but it was sort of a miracle. I was speaking to a group of law students recently and I said it was a really stupid risk to take. And then we didn't get elected and I went on to my articles….

So anyway, I think perhaps because the party had been impressed by the fact that I had done that little kamikaze run in Vancouver Centre, I was asked to go and work for Premier Bill Bennett. That's when I realized I'm not really cut out to be a political staffer. Political staffers are wonderful, and every politician is lucky to have great people work for them. But I realized I'd like to be the hands-on person.

When Premier Bennett decided to step down, I actually ran for the leadership and, no, I didn't win. But in a way I did win because it really elevated my profile. I ran for the legislature in the election that followed, and I was elected. But I didn't get along very well with Bill Vander Zalm, who was the premier. I did some interesting things. I chaired a task force on heritage conservation that took me all around the province. British Columbia by that time was getting to be an age where we were starting to lose some of our heritage buildings. I travelled around the province with a really interesting group of people, and we wrote a report, which later became a white paper that was the basis of the very first legislation for heritage protection in British Columbia. I chaired the justice and legal affairs committee of the legislature, and we went out around the province to conduct hearings. And these were people for whom speaking in public was the thing they feared most in life. The last thing they wanted to do was actually come and talk at a meeting. But what you find is, if you ask somebody to talk about something they know, they're very articulate—you get people talking and say, "Well, what would happen if this? And what do you think about that?" They'll give you great answers and you learn so much. And that was a really powerful thing for me, the opportunity actually to meet with people. I think that one of the most delightful things about being involved in democratic politics is this opportunity to learn about your society. You learn that politics isn't an abstract exercise. Real flesh-and-blood people are affected by what you do. If you go out and you meet with them, you'll learn a lot and you'll probably avoid making a lot of mistakes....

I gained that experience in the provincial legislature. I was there for two years, then I resigned to run federally in 1988. I was never going to be in Vander Zalm's cabinet. The free trade agreement was the big issue. But I learned a lot. The school board and the legislature helped to create my political instincts and reflexes. In local government you don't go someplace else to serve your constituents. They're right there. Many of the decisions you make affect people right away. I think local government is a great place to learn democratic politics because you do everything. You do budgeting. You do labour relations. You do policy. You see the whole realm of what it is that a government does. You learn the relationship between those decisions and the lives of people, whether it's people with children with learning disabilities trying to get the best services for their children or people with potholes in their streets or zoning concerns or whatever. All these things really draw you close to the people and help you to understand what democratic governance is. Those experiences were incredibly valuable to me because then, in 1988, I realized I couldn't go much farther with the premier. We didn't really care for each other. I had been asked a number of times to run in Vancouver Centre for the Progressive Conservatives and I kept saying, "No, no, no." But then, a month or so later the campaign was already on, and three weeks into the campaign I was nominated as a candidate for Vancouver Centre. We started behind but gradually picked up and, just in time for election day, we crossed. I won by 269 votes, but if it had been the next day I'd have won by more. We were moving in the right direction. It was a very interesting campaign, and we had some really good discussions. The local cable station scheduled a debate only among the three candidates on the Canada-US Free Trade Agreement. They kept running them because I think people felt they were good explanations of the different perspectives. In Ottawa, people were aware of this, and a lot of people in the prime minister's team thought that my involvement in the campaign had actually helped other candidates as well. So, when I was elected, I had already come to the attention of the prime minister. I went off to Ottawa and....

KATE GRAHAM: Can you go back a...?

KIM CAMPBELL: I'm a master of the thirty-minute sound bite.

KATE GRAHAM: [laughs] Well, there are a few parts I'm particularly interested in. At every step of your career, you showed signs of leadership—very early on in high school, as valedictorian, as the first female president of your school, and on and on. You took big leaps—running in lots of elections, running for leader very young. You would lose and then just kept on going. Did you feel that perhaps there was something kind of unique about you, or did you feel you had some elevated potential?

KIM CAMPBELL: Well, it's interesting. I guess I knew I was a leader. I didn't think about it like walking around with a little virtual tiara on my head or anything, but I knew that I could mobilize people to do things and that people would support me.

KATE GRAHAM: Okay, but how did you know that?

KIM CAMPBELL: I guess trial and error. I remember one of my colleagues in Parliament told me that he thought I was a born leader. (I once told the story to a reporter who thought I said "boring leader.") Even when I was young, I did feel it was important to break down barriers to girls and women. When I was in Grade 10, a girl had run for student council president, and she didn't win. She was the first girl, I think, even to run. I remember thinking, well that's not right. So, the next year I ran. And I ran against two boys, and I actually got more than half the vote. I used to say that I wanted to be the first woman secretary general of the UN. I was conscious I didn't so much want to be the first woman to be, "Well, how great am I? Bow down," kind of thing. But to break that barrier, this notion that, yes, women can do these things. I liked to make things happen. I've always had a pleasure in empowering other people to do things. I don't have to do them myself; I love to create the circumstances in which other people can do neat things. Whether it's fun things, creative things, world-changing things, whatever. I like to teach and enjoy empowering people with knowledge. As a politician, I think one reason people followed me was because I could explain things. I could explain issues, what was important, and what the choices were. People are perfectly intelligent and can understand anything if you take the trouble to explain it in ways they can [relate to].

KATE GRAHAM: You seem to have a clear sense of self. What you say is trial and error seems to be about seeing that you have this ability to mobilize people around you. And at every stage of your career, it appears that started happening more and more.

KIM CAMPBELL: When I was in high school, I realized that I could move people when I spoke. It frightened me a little. When I was young, I would say to my mother, "How did Hitler come to power?" Because I remember World War II was an 800-pound gorilla in every room. And she said, "Well, he was a very charismatic orator and he got people very excited, and they got carried away with his message." I realized that it carries a huge moral responsibility. When you have the ability to connect with people then you can do great harm as well as great good with it. And that's why I always felt I wanted to do good. I wanted to make people feel positive. I deeply distrust any leader who fundamentally appeals to my anger.

KATE GRAHAM: Okay. I need to ask about when you ran for leader provincially…because that was a very bold move.

KIM CAMPBELL: It was interesting because I found, for some people, the fact that I was much more socially liberal than some members of the party—they actually felt it was important for somebody like me to be running for the leadership. I didn't expect to win.

There were a lot of candidates. I came last. But you know, there was a sense of serendipity. Because at the convention, I was between the two front runners in the lineup of speakers. Everybody stayed tuned and they watched my speech, so the timing couldn't have been better. It was a very good speech. I had learned I could move people and I was a good communicator. And I delivered a very important message: Charisma without substance is a dangerous thing. It creates expectations that cannot be satisfied. Then come bitterness and disillusionment that destroy not only the leader but the party.

It really put me on the map. But when I look back—it was a gutsy thing to do. And I'm sure there are some people who think that it was an arrogant thing to do. I would be perfectly open to people who would think that my deciding to run then or do that then was perhaps not in the best interests of the party. I think, given where the party went, it wouldn't have made that much difference.

KATE GRAHAM: It's funny to think about the turn of events. You ran for a party that did end up putting the first female first minister in place, Rita Johnston. And if you had been successful, maybe we would never have had a woman prime minister in Canada.

KIM CAMPBELL: Yeah. All those things were tough, bare-knuckled political fights. I learned a lot. The one thing I took from all that experience that I think stood me in good stead when I went to Ottawa was that I learned how to work with other people. I didn't always do the right thing, you know. I had to learn to not always say everything I thought. To let other people carry some of the battle. In part, the sense of feeling responsible for things is you think you have to wade in. But it isn't always optimal for you to be the one to wade in. I certainly don't think that my career up to my time in Ottawa was a string of nothing but victories or great things. I also put my foot in my mouth—and happily did it early on in my career—and probably it was good to learn how dumb I could be when the stakes weren't too high.

KATE GRAHAM: Okay, so let's talk about federal politics. You were elected and then were given a number of significant portfolios. What was the experience like, as a woman?

KIM CAMPBELL: It was kind of mixed. On the one hand, politics is a meritocracy in the sense that if you get yourself elected, you're entitled to be there. Nobody can say, "Who are you, mere woman?" Well, yeah, I may be a mere woman, but I got elected. So, when I went to Ottawa, we had to have sessions right away to pass the Canada-US Free Trade Agreement so it could go into force by January 1st. That was interesting because the House had done away with night sittings, but because they needed to get all this business through, they restored night sittings for a short time, which for a brand-new member of Parliament was fun because you could sit around in the parliamentary dining room with the old veterans and hear their war stories. For that particular brief period, it was kind of fun. And then in January, I get a call saying the prime minister would like to see me in Ottawa on Sunday. I mean, it's clear you're going to be invited to be in Cabinet. I flew down to Ottawa. I'm very tired. I went with my husband, and we wound up taking the red eye to get there in time to be available for a meeting on Sunday. I get there and I'm very, very tired and I get a call saying the prime minister will see you at seven. And by this, I thought they meant seven the next morning. My father had come down. He'd said, "I don't want to miss this." So, I met with my husband and my father in Ottawa, and I said, "Let's go and get something to eat." When we came back, the phone is ringing off the hook. "Where are you? The prime minister has asked the RCMP to look for you." I see my life flashing before my eyes. "Oh, seven o'clock tonight?!" My big chance to go to Cabinet. The prime minister, who was staying at Harrington Lake, called me and said, "We should be having this conversation in person." I felt like such a dolt! Imagine, not showing up for a meeting with the prime minister! Anyway, he told me he was going to name me minister of state for Indian affairs and northern development. Once I was sworn in, I brought the senior officials into my office, and I said we need to reinvigorate and restart the discussions on comprehensive land claims in British Columbia. And they said, "Oh, well, you know, BC benefits more from that. They should be doing it." And I said, "Well, I've actually looked into this (it was the last issue I researched for Premier Bennett before he retired) and there is nothing they could do. We have the responsibility. We do a lot of things that benefit one province over another.

And the last I looked, British Columbia was part of Canada." And they went, "Oh." That started the process that resulted in creating the treaty commission in British Columbia....

I didn't complete the process in the year that I was in that portfolio but after that, I was named into justice, and I became the political minister for British Columbia. But it was also a wonderful experience. I travelled around the country and went to a lot of small First Nations communities, and they always treated me with such kindness and respect and good humour. And we'd been building on a lot of law through the courts on righting some of the wrongs on the paternalism of the *Indian Act* regimes in this country. I learned a great deal from that.

KATE GRAHAM: Did it make a difference, you being a woman in this role?

KIM CAMPBELL: Oh, I don't know. Just as cognitive diversity is very important no matter where it comes from, I think the reality of life as women live it often teaches you different lessons, gives you different kinds of perspectives and sensibilities. You see some things that may go unnoticed by somebody who doesn't have to ever justify his right to participate. There's just a different way you think of things when your right to be there hasn't always been accepted. You become sensitive to the disadvantages and challenges that other people face. It's interesting from there to go to a broader view for a minute: one of the things that is really interesting to me is history. Our history is a reflection of who and what we think is important at any given time. It is not a reflection of accomplishment, excellence, innovation, courage. Because all the people who show excellence and accomplishment and innovation and courage who are not the people that we are interested in recognizing, their stories don't get told. And now people are starting to resurrect those stories. I went to the Victoria Forum, after the Truth and Reconciliation Commission. The BC Lieutenant Governor was talking about the residential schools and the treatment of the First Nations. There are lots of Canadians who have no idea that First Nations people were in uniform in World War II and were treated like garbage when they came back. They hoped it would be an avenue toward a more equal citizenship, and it wasn't. We idealize all the other nice, white, young men who went off, including my father, but we leave out a whole bunch who didn't look like that, who did the same thing. Our history is so much more interesting and so much more multicoloured and multigendered than we understand. If we want to have a more diverse and inclusive future, then we have to have a more diverse and inclusive history....

But going back again to this question of women. When I was young, I was an anomaly for some reason or other. I thought if I wanted to lead, I should be able to lead, and I just kind of pushed my way forward. And I did encounter sexism. Then some people are afraid you'll get special treatment. But for a lot of women, if you were seen as an anomaly, it was easier because you didn't have the baggage that people thought you were the thin edge of a wedge that was going to really change things. Take Margaret Thatcher. She wasn't all that helpful to other women. I think she liked to think, they could all be like me if they wanted to be. She didn't see the particularities of her own situation.

KATE GRAHAM: Let's turn to the chapter of your seeking federal leadership and then your time as prime minister. Brian Mulroney runs into some issues and so on, and you probably had a sense that there was a change coming in the party. When did it first dawn on you to think about seeking the leadership?

KIM CAMPBELL: When I was in my first cabinet portfolio, minister of state for Indian affairs, I used to give talks about the Meech Lake Accord. I remember I was invited that year to speak to the big PC Canada Fund dinner in Winnipeg. They used to have a huge dinner for the Manitoba Progressive Conservatives, federal and provincial, in Winnipeg every year. I was asked to be their keynote speaker. Sometimes I'd get invited to go and speak to a riding association. And people would come up to me and say, "When Mulroney steps down, you're gonna be our next leader."

KATE GRAHAM: Who is "people?"

KIM CAMPBELL: Just people in ridings. I'd go to speak at these ridings and people, after they'd heard me, would come over and say, "When Brian Mulroney steps down, you're going to be our next leader." And I remember saying it was kind of embarrassing because I didn't think the prime minister was going anywhere and I'm not looking to fill a job in which there isn't a vacancy. And I remember he said to me, "I think you're going to lead this party and I think it's just going to happen naturally." I mean it was very interesting that he saw that I was not aiming to do that. But what struck me is that others saw that in me....

I was in fact very careful never to create any sense that I was creating a leadership campaign. It would have seemed very disloyal from my perspective. But people were beginning to talk about [whether] Mulroney would step down because we were going through difficult things when the Charlottetown Accord failed. And people would come up to my staff and say, "If Kim runs for leader, put me down. I want to support her." And we'd say, "We have no campaign." But what was clear was that people saw me as a very viable candidate and I think being justice minister had really raised my profile. I had dealt with a lot of very difficult issues, and I dealt with them in ways that didn't alienate my colleagues, even the ones who didn't agree with me. And I think I built a relationship of trust with a lot of people who knew that even if they didn't agree with me, I would treat them with respect. I would include them. I wouldn't play fast and loose with things. Even knowing they might not win the argument, they would be okay with me and would get as much input as they would with anybody....

I remember in November of 1992, [Ray,] my former chief of staff, wrote a memo to me on what it would mean to run for the leadership. Ray wanted me to be very clear about what was involved and what it would mean.

KATE GRAHAM: Turned out to be quite a timely note.

KIM CAMPBELL: Yeah, because there was a lot of discussion about it. But then Ray said, "Well, the prime minister is meeting with the campaign team. If the prime minister meets with the campaign team next week, he can't step down. He can't create a campaign team and then not be the person who leads the campaign." He thought for sure that Brian Mulroney would stay. And oddly enough, it's interesting, I think if Brian Mulroney had stayed we would have done better. I don't think we'd have won in '93. I think we'd have done better because when an unpopular leader steps down, it makes it very difficult for those who follow him. I never criticized him during the '93 campaign. But he had become the most unpopular prime minister in the history of Canadian polling. It was very, very difficult. If he had been leading us, he could have taken Jean Chrétien head on. And whether he would have succeeded in winning or not, I think we'd have done better. Then would have been the time to step down to choose a new leader....

But the problem was, by stepping down as late as he did, we had no time to put a new face on the government. He stepped down but we were already halfway through the fifth year of a mandate. Normally, you never even go into the fifth year of a mandate. There was no time for a successor, no matter whom it had been, to put a new face on the party. And finding your positioning with respect to the previous government or the government that you served in and what you wanted to do, it was very, very difficult. It was the worst situation....

Ray stepped down to become the chair of my campaign. We reached out and found out that almost two-thirds of the caucus supported me. And so again, how can you not run? That was really quite amazing. The prime minister wanted a contest. But none of the other senior ministers could get the support that they needed to run a campaign. Maybe some of them blamed me. But the point is, Brian Mulroney really didn't want a coronation. And yet by creating a very contentious leadership campaign, it weakened me to fight that campaign and distracted energy and resources from preparing for a general election. Perrin Beatty, I think, had wanted to be prime minister since he was old enough to know what it was, but he decided not to run because he said, "The party wants Kim, and the only way I can run against her is to damage her." He got it and put the interests of the party above his own dreams of possibly being prime minister. But we had been in power for two mandates. And a lot of things had happened: Two unsuccessful attempts to amend the Constitution, the Canada-US Free Trade Agreement, the Goods and Services Tax, all this stuff. And so, there were a lot of levers for people to pull to attack us. But I think the campaign itself was a very interesting example of what sexism looks like. Although it's hard to parse it out because people are perfectly entitled not to like us as a party and to be mad at us and whatever. But what you see and what the research shows—I have now read it and hadn't at the time. If it had existed at the time, I might have been able to be better prepared. The fundamental truth was that you never get the benefit of the doubt if you are not the prototypical leader. If you don't look or sound like the other people who've done it, there is no benefit of the doubt. People would say things like, "Kim Campbell said such and such and we jumped all over her. Jean Chrétien said the same thing and we left him alone. Gee, that Jean Chrétien sure can manipulate the media." But he wasn't manipulating the media. He belonged. He was infinitely forgivable. People didn't think I belonged—particularly in the press gallery, who had been covering prime ministers for a long time. I didn't look and sound like any of the previous ones. We've learned a lot now about the research on social and cognitive psychology, about cognitive biases, both in terms of how we think but also in how we evaluate people and implicit attitudes and why diversity is so difficult to actually create.

KATE GRAHAM: We talk a lot now about the glass cliff. At the time, did you think the election was winnable? And did you think that being a woman would be a benefit, electorally?

KIM CAMPBELL: Well, whenever you campaign you always have to believe you can win. You simply could never get out of bed in the morning and do it. There has to be a certain amount of what I call constructive denial. But there were a number of things. In the summer of 1993, Gallup said that I had in a brief period the highest approval rate of any prime minister in thirty years. Which included all of the Trudeau years. That gives you a kind of hope. I think people liked me. But there are a whole lot of other factors that are part of it. We had two parties running, the Reform Party in the West and the Bloc Québécois in the East, who couldn't possibly form a government. And so, you think, how can people in Québec vote for the Bloc? Because we'd always thought Québec strategically voted for the parties that would put them in government so they would have power. And voting for the Bloc guaranteed they wouldn't have power. The same thing with the Reform Party. I mean it was a regional party, they didn't run candidates all over the country. There's no way they could form a government. They could only be spoilers. I actually kept our base across the country, but I couldn't keep our Québec vote, which wasn't our base. It was the vote that Brian Mulroney had brought into the party successfully. And Lucien Bouchard had absconded with it. I remember when he resigned and went off to create the Bloc Québécois. My caucus colleagues from Québec would come into caucus and say, "The Bloc has nominated a complete nonentity in my riding and he's already running ahead of me." The Reform Party—I think Preston Manning has a lot to answer for. I think he's a very destructive figure in Canadian politics because he doesn't play with anybody else's ball and bat. His whole way of dividing and hiving off the conservative vote in Alberta and the West was to portray members of Parliament as [being] at the trough, all that kind of stuff, which was incredibly unfair and untrue. It's almost like it didn't really have anything to do with a rational calculation of what it would mean. People didn't like Brian Mulroney; maybe they wanted a change. And although there were some people who liked me a lot, it's easy to raise a doubt about somebody. Like Hillary Clinton: people say, "Well, I'll vote for a woman but not that woman." In spite of all of that, 66 million people there cast their ballots for her.

KATE GRAHAM: Let's talk about that. When you became leader and prime minister, there was enormous excitement about finally seeing a woman in this role. They see someone different in the role and they want things to fundamentally change. It didn't take long though before there were protests, "Kim, Kim, she's just like him." How did it feel to be, and have the weight of being, the first female prime minister? What were the expectations you could feel upon you and how did you handle them?

KIM CAMPBELL: Well, it would be the same way if you were Québécois or if you were First Nations or whatever. Nobody can deliver. Even as prime minister, you can't deliver on a whole agenda.

You're still governing a whole country. And not everybody wants the same things. And so, your role is to try to identify the things that are in the national interest that you can deliver on. I wasn't afraid the day I was sworn in as justice minister at Rideau Hall. I came out and was interviewed and I described myself as a feminist, and there was an audible intake of breath from coast to coast, but people got over it. When you're prime minister, it was a big deal. But that didn't mean that I could immediately turn around and deliver on a feminist agenda or even if that would be appropriate for me to do as prime minister. When I was running for the leadership, I produced a document about doing politics. I forget the actual title of it, but I had, in the course of being a minister, been struck by how hard it is for government backbenchers to communicate the extent to which they are representing their constituents. Like when I was [doing] my gun control [legislation], some of my colleagues didn't support it and they had their teeth in my ankles. And they were doing their job. They were doing what their constituents wanted. But whereas opposition members can take public pot shots, government members are supposed to argue behind the scenes and then you come to agreements, and you do it. And that's fine for issues that are part of your electoral mandate, that if you run on a platform, I think you're entitled to ask your colleagues to support it. But [when] things come up [that are] unanticipated, I think that it's not necessary to ask everybody to support it. And I always negotiated dissent with my colleagues and said, "[If] you're going to vote against or you want to abstain, you want to be out of the House." I understood that for some of them on some of the issues, particularly the gun control one, that they couldn't support them.

I had written this document about various ways in which it would actually empower government backbenchers. And I thought the importance of it was that it would address some of the cynicism people felt about party politics. I had a little press conference, and I released a document and then one reporter said, "Yeah, but what do you really stand for?" And I thought, "Oh, just shoot me...." I mean this was probably one of the most radical views of how to use prime ministerial power. If a tree falls in the forest and nobody hears it, is there any sound? If a prime minister makes a statement and no journalist understands it, is there any coverage of it? If it's not something that people see as important? And yet it could be the kind of thing that ordinary people relate to because it addresses their own sense of whether the system is working for them or not....

When I became prime minister, I redesigned the ministries of government because I wanted to make Cabinet smaller. I actually think that it was a very good design, if I do say so myself. Not that much of it has survived but it meant I also had to change the deputies because I was reducing the number of ministries. It also meant reducing the number of deputy ministers and reappointing them. I discovered that the women deputies were very unhappy and felt that women had been appointed to the more marginal posts. And I must confess, I just hadn't had time to really look at that. And I was also just trying to get us through an election on the theory that if we won then we could go back more seriously to the drawing board and really look at how to do that. But it kind of took me by surprise and I realized that this was something where you had to keep your eye on the ball for that all the time. And I couldn't be so different from my predecessors that I was unrecognizable, or I wouldn't be supported as prime minister. So, you're damned if you do, damned if you don't. You don't look or sound like any of the other ones, but if you get too different, you're not credible in the role because they have defined the role. The first non-prototypical leader carries that burden....

I did my best. But there was so little time that we had to go to an election so quickly. And again, the time was spent running a very contentious leadership campaign rather than spending that time mapping out a strategy for going to the people. Could we have won? Maybe not. But we might have done better, and we might have avoided some difficulties. I don't know. What was good about being the first woman prime minister was it clearly meant a lot to a lot of people. The excitement of people, men and women. And even now, you know I was out of Canada for a long time, and when I came back to do that project at the University of Alberta people would say to me, "You know, I was eight when you became prime minister. It was such a big deal." "I was in university, and I just remember it so well. I remember, you know, we watched and how excited we were." And they don't say, "And then when you lost, we thought it was game over." They remember that excitement, they see that. And that's important to me because it was a big deal. There are also people who tweet and say, "Well, you were prime minister for ten minutes." My husband gets mad. He says, "I guess your wife was busy that weekend?" [laughs] But if you look back, it's been twenty-six years now. And nobody else has done it. And it's not because there aren't good people out there but it's because it's harder than it looks. Women get to be leaders of parties that don't have a chance of forming government. Audrey McLaughlin was leader of the NDP, and I don't for a nanosecond mean to take anything away from her. She's a very smart and able person. But the fight for the position is much harder when somebody thinks you might actually be prime minister.

KATE GRAHAM: In the '93 campaign, when do you recall first knowing that you were in trouble?

KIM CAMPBELL: We knew we were in trouble. But the Chrétien ads—John Tory, who was campaign chair, called us and said, "We're gonna do some ads tomorrow that are a bit negative, and you may hear something from that. But we use a picture that was sort of like the picture used on *Maclean's* magazine." And doesn't tell me what's in the ads. He suggested I might hear something. The next morning I heard something, people talking about this image of the Chrétien campaign. And I understood it was a picture that was used on the cover of *Maclean's* magazine. Whatever, whatever. It's not till the end of that day when I talked to people in my own riding and they said, "Look, people are tearing up their lawn signs." I said, "You gotta pull the ads." But I didn't see them until the end of the day when somebody got me a VHS. I was in a hotel in Montréal. Remember that we didn't have that ability to communicate really fast, so I couldn't see them until somebody could give me a video of them. And when I saw it, my first reaction was, "Whose side are they are on? How could anybody produce that ad and think that I would approve it?" I inherited a campaign team, and I had no time to pick my own campaign team. And to this day some think I was wrong to pull the ads. We actually had a bounce in our polling with it. It is true that negative ads can work. But the problem is they don't work for women, women get blamed for them. But it just was also—it was just so tone deaf and stupid. The interesting thing is that Jean Chrétien knows perfectly well I had nothing to do with those ads. His nephew, Raymond Chrétien, visited me when he was our ambassador in Washington and I was consul general in Los Angeles and I said, "Those ads—I had nothing to do with them." He said, "If you had, you wouldn't be here."

We were trying to have a campaign that recognized that I was a woman. Some of the women who supported me were trying to get events with women and they couldn't get through to me. Finally, we did a big event in Toronto with women in business and it was a huge success. These women are all saying, "Oh, if only we'd known." But it was like the campaign was afraid to capitalize on the fact that I was a woman. It was like a Brian Mulroney campaign, only for me. And you say, "Well, why didn't you do something?" I did as much as I could, but the problem is you can't run your own campaign. I was sworn in on the 25th of June and we had to drop the writ at the beginning of September. I was exhausted and I just wanted a few days just to rest. And every time we booked some time for me to rest, well, you have to do this, and you have to do that. And we need to do this interview and do that. There was never any time. I remember getting to the point where I was so tired that I kind of…I felt kind of futile. It took away a lot of my hope. The thing that restores the hope is actually meeting with people. When you meet with people, you campaign, and you actually shake hands with the people, that actually…there's almost like there's an infusion of energy into you. It tires you in the sense that at the end your adrenaline stops pumping, but it is one of the few things that helps to keep your balance. It was a very, very hard campaign. After the leadership campaign—the day after I was elected leader of the party at the convention—I met with the clerk of the Privy Council, Glen Shortliffe, who came with a binder of all the promises I had made as a leadership candidate and proposals for how to realize them. I'm sure he had a similar binder for Jean Chrétien, Jean Charest, and the others. In other words, he was paying attention to what I was saying so that if I was elected leader, they could immediately serve me by helping me to implement the things that I wanted to implement. But John Tory, who was the campaign chair, said when I met him, "Oh, he hadn't really been paying much attention to the campaign, the leadership campaign, because he wanted to remain neutral so that he could serve whoever won." I thought, remaining neutral doesn't mean being detached. Neutral means being prepared to run a campaign for whichever of the leading candidates wins. The clerk of the Privy Council, who is totally nonpartisan, it is only there to serve the government, saw it as his job to prepare to serve whomever won. But the campaign chair didn't. I was absolutely flabbergasted. But where do you go?

In July of 1993...I saw Mulroney after the election, who was now the former prime minister. I went to see him in Montréal as a courtesy call after the election. And he said, "Oh, you know, the party didn't serve you well." I thought, "Oh, really?" And he said, "And I was at an event, and somebody said to me, when I saw that so-and-so was doing the advertising campaign, I knew we were in trouble." I thought, "Really, you wouldn't tell me this? You know, these are your people that you hand-picked, and I had a little over two months between being anointed as prime minister and having to call the election. And in between that, doing a G7 summit and travelling across the country to the UN to speak at the General Assembly. I had to do all those things in that brief period before the election was called. You know, it wasn't really optimal." When you're campaigning it brings up more of the need to be adversarial and that's harder for a woman to pull off, I think. The adversarial nature of an election campaign is not as congenial to people's expectations of how women should be. It's harder to carry it off.

KATE GRAHAM: Going through the experience of losing elections has got to be one of the toughest moments that there is in Canadian politics—and I suspect even harder when you are the prime minister at the time. What was that experience like for you?

KIM CAMPBELL: As a woman, I was to blame for it all. Like Hillary Clinton, who people say was a flawed candidate. And I say, wait a minute, wait a minute, she got 66 million votes. She might not have been perfect, but she was amazing. Don't dismiss her loss by saying she was a flawed candidate. She was a great candidate. To describe her as a flawed candidate is such...compared to whom? It's just mind-boggling. It's that "success has many fathers; failure is an orphan" kind of thing. I'm perfectly prepared to admit that I made mistakes....

I remember a year before the election, I was at a charity auction in Vancouver with my friend and we bid on a stay in a little spot called the Oaks in California, which is owned by a Canadian. When we bought it, her husband said, "I have a feeling that you won't be available to use that." And, of course, if we won the election I wouldn't have. When I lost the election my friend said, "Well, the bad news is you lost the election. The good news is our stay at the Oaks is good till December 1st. Do you want to go?" So, we went out. I was there for a week. And when I came back, there was an article in the Vancouver *Sun* that referred to rumours that I had had a nervous breakdown. People thought that somehow I was going to come apart, you know? But in my life—my mother left when I was twelve and I didn't see her for ten years—and what I went through then was a loss so much greater than the election loss in '93. The election loss in '93 was awful. It was devastating because I loved being a politician and I thought I was good at it. Of all the things I've done in my life I think it's the thing I'm best at because it combines a lot of things that I both can do and like to do. I was dating this guy, Gregory, and there were rumours that supposedly he had been travelling on the campaign with me. But, no, he hadn't. The only person who travelled with me was my stepdaughter. Do you really think I'm stupid enough to think I could have carted around a guy throughout the campaign, and nobody would have noticed? There were these stories that I supposedly had this insatiable sexual relationship with somebody. But Gregory came out on election day and busied himself until it was time to count the votes. I remember that night we actually had a big fight because I knew that it meant the end of my career. And he refused to believe it because he wasn't very sophisticated about politics. And it just annoyed me that he was in denial about it. But I wasn't wallowing. First of all, I would never give the naysayers the satisfaction of not coping. Why would you ever allow these jerks who never gave you the benefit of the doubt, who were always giving you a hard time, why would you give them the satisfaction of falling apart? And besides, I had suffered pain in my life. I had suffered loss. And I had come through it and there was no question to me that I would survive. But there was no point in saying, no, I'm not devastated. Yes, for me it was devastating and terrible, but it was not the end of the world. And I wasn't stupid because of it. I wasn't lacking in ability. It may have been that people wanted to justify it—that I was a flawed candidate. They did it with Hillary Clinton. But the fact of the matter is I knew I was able to do things and I just had to find how I could pursue the things that mattered to me in my life in ways that didn't involve being prime minister of Canada.

KATE GRAHAM: Did you find it tough to kind of reconnect with the sense of your own identity? I mean, it's such a defining role.

KIM CAMPBELL: I wasn't in it long enough for it to define me. That may be one way in which women are different from men. I shouldn't say this because there's probably research for it, but I think that women are perhaps less encouraged to identify themselves by their professions than men are by what they do for a living. It was a wonderful accomplishment, but I never saw it as burned into my skin, that this was integral to me. In my life, there were things where I was in the right place at the right time and some places ahead of my time. I may have been ahead of my time. But I think what's important is that I wasn't over my head. I knew what I was doing. But I didn't get a chance to do it as long as I would have liked. I've often thought, you know, I wonder how it would have worked out for me? I'd already had marriages come to an end. I wonder how I would have managed. I remember saying to Gregory, "If I'd won, I wouldn't be able to have a relationship with you." He got very upset about that. I said, "No, I would not. I would have had to manage my personal life very differently." I knew that and that might have been a hard thing to deal with. Pierre Trudeau was a single man before he married Margaret. That was fine. But I think for a woman it might have been more difficult. Maybe I missed having to deal with that. I don't know. But I would hope that women looking at my experience would recognize that a woman certainly can do it. It's not easy to get that power and nobody is going to give it to you. But if you think you would exercise it ethically and in the national interest, why shouldn't it be you?

KATE GRAHAM: Looking back, do you feel you were set up to fail?

KIM CAMPBELL: I don't think I was being set up to fail. I think there is a certain Hail Mary pass that when you know you're in trouble you try to find somebody who is the same only different to lead you. And the idea that by having Canada's first female prime minister you might get a leg up on what was going to be a very difficult political fight, I think was attractive. But I also think that there may be some people who are less concerned that if you're a female then you fail. That that confirms some deep sense that they have that maybe women aren't really cut out for this. A lot of people have said to me—a lot of women have said to me—that was Mulroney's loss, and you were set up to take Mulroney's loss. In other words, that he was the leader who had created the problem with the political following and that he didn't want to take it on. I don't think there's any question that he didn't want to lose an election. I think if he had stayed, we would have done better. I don't think we would have won. He did something that no Conservative leader had done since Sir John A. Macdonald, to win two back-to-back majority governments. And I think he wanted to go out as a winner. And when it was clear that he wasn't going to be able to, he waited as long as possible. He didn't want to leave right after the Charlottetown Accord because that was a loss. If that had passed, I think he probably would have announced his retirement right after. I don't begrudge him wanting to go out as a winner. I don't begrudge him that personal calculus. I think it also, however, got in the way of him being candid about what the difficulties were. He kept saying, "Well, we had policy and we had money and we were all ready to go. I've set the bar. I've left the party a great situation." Well, no, he didn't. And we didn't need that BS. I mean a more realistic assessment of the problem we were facing would have been helpful....

I don't expect people to be superhuman. Nobody is as bad as their worst critic thinks or as good as their biggest fan thinks. What's interesting about people is the combination of their strengths and weaknesses. And I don't waste my time being mad at people for being human because I hope people will forgive me for being human. I've got feet of clay up to my neck, too. I have my naysayers out there, particularly some of these gems from the current Conservative party who say, "You were prime minister for ten minutes. You're the worst prime minister and the biggest failure in Canadian politics." I wasn't, actually. But if it makes you feel good to think that, you go for it, honey....

I don't think I had time to set out an agenda of what I wanted to do as the first female prime minister. Had we won the election, I might have been able to do that. But I was very aware, and I was very warmed by the extent to which being the first female prime minister clearly seemed to matter. I've seen pictures of me shaking young women's hands and you can see how excited they are. It's because they see in me a possibility for their own lives and perhaps a validation for their own lives. Little old men used to come up to me and go, "Oh, you're going to be our Maggie Thatcher." And I thought, well, this is interesting. She has created a constituency for a man who will vote for women that we never dreamed of. I think of the night of the convention, when I won, and one of my supporters, with tears running down his cheeks, said, "This is for my daughter." I think I was very conscious of what it meant to people. And what it could mean to people. And had I had a chance to govern longer, I think I would have looked for even more concrete ways to hold on to that change in Canadian history. It's a source of great pleasure to me to have been the instrument of that feeling among young women. I thought, this is what I'd really like, for people to feel they could stand on my shoulders in the sense that I stood on the shoulders of people who went before, Flora MacDonald and others who were quite remarkable and, incidentally, also certainly survived not being able to get the job they wanted to get. To be a vehicle that gives people a sense of possibility, it's just a great privilege.

EVA AARIAK

PREMIER OF NUNAVUT
(2008-2013)

Throughout Canada's history, most of our political leaders have fit a concerningly similar mould: older, white, and male; extroverts with a dominant and effusive personality; an affluent upbringing, and usually entering politics through business or law.

Eva Aariak doesn't fit this mould.

The petite Inuk woman has a distinctly different vibe. She is quiet and soft-spoken with a kind and patient nature that shines through within moments of meeting her. Perhaps even more importantly, she leaves the person she is speaking to with a distinct impression that, along with her many political accomplishments, she has never forgotten who she is or where she came from.

Aariak was born in a camp outside Arctic Bay, a small Inuit hamlet on the northern shores of Baffin Island. Her family moved into the community when she was a young girl so she could attend school. What followed was a remarkable professional and political career that included working as an educator, a journalist, an entrepreneur, and then as an elected official.

In 1999, the new territory of Nunavut was formed from the vast northern and eastern portion of the Northwest Territories. The sparsely populated territory is one of the world's largest subnational territories, home to a population of fewer than 40,000 people. Aariak, age forty-four at the time, became by appointment the new territory's first languages commissioner. She served in this role for five years, working to protect Indigenous language rights across services and sectors as the new territorial government was being formed. One of her most noted contributions in this role was determining the Inuktitut word for the Internet, choosing *ikiaqqivik*, which aptly means travelling through layers.

Aariak was elected to the Nunavut Legislative Assembly in 2008, the only woman. Under Nunavut's consensus government model, the unicameral and nonpartisan legislative assembly selects a premier from among elected members at a leadership forum held shortly after the election. The premier then selects the cabinet. That year, the incumbent premier wanted to stay in the role, but the newly elected Aariak was voted in by secret ballot, making her the first (and to date, only) female premier of Nunavut.

Aariak spent five years in this role. In 2018, she was named a member of the Order of Canada for her accomplishments and contributions. In 2021, Prime Minister Justin Trudeau named Aariak as the commissioner of Nunavut, a governor-in-council appointment to fulfill many of the duties similar to those of lieutenant governors in the provinces.

Aariak and I met between these significant posts, after her service as premier but before the news of her appointment as commissioner was announced. I recall thinking when we met that Canada and the world needed more leaders like Aariak—soft-spoken and kind-hearted, with a clear vision and commitment to equity and protecting the rights of the people she served. In reading her story, I think you'll see why.

"Women have that ability to see the big picture. And, in my case, I looked to the future." Eva Aariak was elected premier by her peers in Nunavut's consensus legislature.

EVA AARIAK: I was born in a camp outside of Arctic Bay, before Arctic Bay was populated. My parents and myself and my older sister moved into Arctic Bay when I was about five, when we moved into my grandfather's house. It was a one-room house, and it was only the second Inuit home there. There was a Hudson's Bay Company store. There was one teacher and a one-room classroom. I tried going to school shortly after we moved back with my cousins. I was the only child of my age at the time and the next one was three years younger than I was. We would play with each other outside while our cousins and his sisters and brothers were in school. One day I guess they were feeling sorry for me. "Why don't you just go into the school and see what happens?" So, I said, "Okay." I didn't even tell my mother that I was walking to the school with them. I walked in and the teacher says, "No." From her expression and her gesture I understood, although I didn't speak one word of English. She said, "No, next year." I had to leave the school, but I was ready at the time, you know? In retrospect sometimes I think, "Why didn't you even let me colour books or something like that?" [laughs] But that was Arctic Bay. It was very small. Through my time growing up, it grew from the sixties with prefabricated homes. Families that were in the outlying camps moved in mainly because they were asked to move back into the centre in Arctic Bay so that their children could go to school and so on. They left their livelihood where they were completely self-sufficient by hunting and living the way they've always lived....

Throughout the years as I was growing up, I witnessed the community. I also saw some of the community members and the professionals, such as the teachers and even some Hudson's Bay Company employees, doing community work. It was very evident when the community was so very small that the little things that are done by people are making a little difference. For instance, our teacher was a photographer. He taught photography and developing films to adults in the evening while his wife, who was not a teacher, helped the women. They had to wash their clothing by hand at home. She would open the school on the weekend and have the washing machine and everything. It was a place where the women would go and do all their laundry and things like that, you know. From that point, when I was very young, I saw the community involvement and the way that helps make life easier. One of our Hudson's Bay Company clerks was our gym teacher. Our wonderful teacher didn't have the skills in gymnastics, but he felt that exercise and gymnastics were important. He was being resourceful with what you have in the community….

In retrospect, I think growing up with that, I feel strongly how community, working together, is so important. We have our own social workers per se. These are our elders and adults who would help each other with mental health. And if one's family passes away then they are totally taken care of by the elders in the community. And child-rearing practices: I had my first child at age twenty-three. I had a lot of support in terms of child-rearing practices and learning from the experiences that other woman had with their own first child. These kinds of things were still very strong at the time, which unfortunately today are not as readily available because, you know, we live in different places. We have our own homes. We're not engaged with our elders as closely as we used to be. Because of a lot of other things, work and so on, being away from your own home community, from your relatives….

I went away to school and then I went back home. I was interested in being a member of the recreation committee. That was my very first real introduction [to community involvement]. My drive was the fact that there were no recreational activities organized as I thought they should be. One day I made a suggestion that we should shovel off the ice because we live right next to the ocean, shovel off the area where people can skate and enjoy outdoors. I approached the hamlet council. I went in as a delegate and requested that one of those snow-plowing machines clear an area for skating. They went in camera and told me to wait outside and, not too long later, I went back in, and they said, "Unfortunately, we can't do that." And that was that. I went back to the committee, and I told them what happened. But one of the hamlet employees who was the heavy equipment operator, he just went out to the ice and did it anyway. He knew how important it was. [laughs] So we had our skating rink….

These things developed and over time I became involved in education committees and health committees, recreation committees, and hamlet councillor when I was in another community, in Pond Inlet. I was involved early on in the small politics, per se, as a community member. And when we moved into another community, Iqaluit, where I live now; I was involved in the education committee, the museum board. You know, different boards and so on. That really helped me take these as stepping stones to the political arena. When I was asked if I was interested in being a candidate for a member of legislature, I had thought about it before. I've always kept myself, to a large degree, informed on what's happening politically. If I can't be watching the debates, political debates, I'd be listening to them on the radio. I'd stay up late because the election results wouldn't be announced sometimes until after midnight, not really knowing or not really having a thought that I want to be there one day. But I think that subconsciously, maybe I did? Maybe not. I'm not sure. When I was asked…deep down, I knew this was something that I wanted to do. It just didn't come out. So, when I was asked, you know, then I said yes. I approached my immediate family. I was a single parent then, so that had to be considered as well. And yeah, I got in. [laughs]

KATE GRAHAM: Tell me a bit about the 2008 election. As I understand it, you were the only woman elected.

EVA AARIAK: Yes. In the elected membership I was the only female.

KATE GRAHAM: Talk to me about what that was like. You're now an elected official and you're the only woman at the table.

EVA AARIAK: You know, when I put my mind to it and I decide that I want to do something, I don't think about my gender. I didn't think, "Oh, I'm the only female member." No. It didn't occur to me right away. What really stood out for me was, "Oh my, I'm elected now. Now the real work starts, the things that I have to do — engaging with people and listening to people." I was more engaged in the role than being the only female elected.

KATE GRAHAM: Was it something that seemed to matter to other people?

EVA AARIAK: It was cited quite often, particularly in the media. Of course, you know, I was very proud and humbled to be elected into that position. And it was only after the election took place and we were in our first orientation session in the legislative assembly that it became more apparent to me when everybody else is sitting around the table and they're all male members from the communities that are elected. And I did notice that. We have a consensus style of government in Nunavut, where the speaker at the legislative assembly is chosen by peers first, and then the premier is selected by peers. I was approached by a couple of people within the legislative assembly members when it was time to select someone for a run for the premiership....

But at that time, I wasn't fully prepared to be going for that position, although I felt that this was something that I could put myself into and try my best. When I was nominated by my peers to be the premier, I thought hard. I talked it over with my family because it's a different role than being a regular member because you are much more engaged in travels and so on. I agreed that I'd be nominated and when the election time came around, I was surprised. There were two other male members that were competing for the same position. I was surprised and very humbled by the results of the vote that took place that day....

I never felt, "Okay, I'm going to make these big changes." I always felt that I was going to help make changes in collaboration with my peers. I think women tend to be more collaborative and they listen and try to understand the issues and everything else around it so that they can make a better choice. Women are caretakers in the home and in their community; we get involved. We have that ability to see the big picture, I think. And in my case, I looked to the future.

KATE GRAHAM: Tell me a bit more about consensus government.

EVA AARIAK: There are only two territories in Canada that are in the model of consensus government, Nunavut and Northwest Territories. Yukon has a political party system. In consensus government, you get elected and then the elected members — all of the elected members — choose their speaker, their premier, their ministers. They are elected by their peers through a secret ballot. So, there is a perpetual minority in the cabinet and the regular members are always in larger numbers. If the members do not agree with what the cabinet is proposing, then they have the power to overturn the cabinet decision. When I go on speaking engagements and explain this consensus-style government, people in the south say, "Wow, that's how everything should be." You know, it's very much connected with our own cultural way of consensus where the majority decision goes. But at the same time, from my own experience in the cabinet, if, as a premier, I may individually approve of what the issue is at hand, because of the consensus and the way it operated, whatever the majority wanted would have to go, even if I as premier did not agree with it. I would try my best to explain why. But, you know, it's the majority that would make the decisions. It has its pros and cons. And I have a feeling that one day in the future, it may change. People are starting to talk a bit about party politics.

KATE GRAHAM: Okay, so even in this model, do you think it was harder for you to take that leap as a woman?

EVA AARIAK: Yes. I have been trying to encourage women to go out there. I usually say just do it when they feel that they are ready. They will know within their heart that if they were put in that position they would try their best. But it is harder for women to release that feeling, saying I want to be there. Because I think women have to gauge where everything is at first. Where they are in the home, in the community, with their children and their responsibilities in the home. Because all of these would be affected. There are so many things, you know, providing meals every day. How would that change? They're doing laundry. How would that change? Women have to consider these little things because many times they are the ones that are doing all these kinds of things. I'm so very proud of men who are taking more of a shared responsibility in the home. I totally applaud that. I see that happening more. But it still needs to be done further — and women still do need more encouraging. I think they also need to see the role models of people who are out there and are doing what they can. And I always said when I was in the position of premiership, I said, "If I can do it, if Eva Aariak can do it, surely, surely you can do it." That was the message. I'm still very much saying that to people—if I can do it then you can do it. Probably even better than I can! There are so many wonderful, inspiring, talented, skillful, strong-minded women out there now, particularly in the area that I live in.

KATE GRAHAM: Do you remember facing any overt or less overt forms of sexism?

EVA AARIAK: There were times that I wondered if the situation would be different if I were a man. At one time I got to a point where I said it to my cabinet members, "I don't think you would be doing that if I were a man." Later, I thought, "Hmm, I wonder if I should have said that?" And who knows what kind of dialogue and so on would happen when I'm not around? But they tried their best to be respectful. I think this is something that is experienced by many women in any level of higher management. But it was never to a point where it was very stressful for me.

KATE GRAHAM: Tell me about your time as premier. What stands out for you as some of your proudest moments?

EVA AARIAK: There were many proud moments. Being selected by all your peers, being the only woman in the legislature. That was a very humbling and honouring feeling. We needed to deal with many of the social issues in our new territory. It's a developing territory with many challenges. And we didn't expect to make changes right from the beginning. It's impossible. You have to take steps in order to make it the way you want to see it, you know; it doesn't happen overnight. And people understand that. But at the same time, many people actually expect that, [saying], "Why isn't it there already?" And to some degree today I understand that. Because I think we should be farther ahead in different areas with education, with social aspects of some of the stuff that needed…that needs to be done. Mental health. We have a high suicide rate. Housing is still very much in need in all of our territories, I think. With my passion in Inuktitut language, in our culture, in addressing social issues, advocating for child and youth position, and things like that. There were moments where I felt good about moving forward. But in four years, how much can you do? Poverty reduction strategies were one of the things that we worked very hard on, that I strongly believed in. I think we set good directions. In our term, it was not going to be finished to a point where we would like but social issues were very important to me. It was also very important to look at the economy. Economic development, I mean, it goes hand in hand. Give the people opportunity to grow and feel grounded and rooted so that they will be strong in moving forward as community members. We are still very much hunter-gatherers. We rely very much on our environment and our animals to feed. The cost of living in Nunavut is very high. And in order to supplement your nutritious meals, you need to go out and hunt. And in order to go out and hunt you have to have the means of buying ammunition, the snowmobiles, all these things. The maintenance of your snow machine. All these things require you to be employed. It's complex. We still have a long way to go in developing our society so that they are feeling that they are supported.

KATE GRAHAM: Your premiership came to an end in 2013. Tell me what that was like for you.

EVA AARIAK: Before our term ended, I announced that I would not be seeking the premiership. I was surprised how the media, like particularly the southern media and so on, really took that on. "What?!" That type of thing. I had been thinking, because of my travel and so much time away from my own constituents, I needed to be closer to my constituency. I ran again after announcing that I would not be seeking the premiership, but I would be seeking membership at the legislature. I was disappointed, of course, with less than fifty votes. But, to me, that was not devastating because I still feel that I can contribute in a way that I need to. Even though you're not in an elected position, you try your best. And so, you do what you have to do and I'm very happy where I am now, working in an Inuit organization. I'm also involved in some other board memberships as well....

When I was a student, we had wonderful counsellors here who were our teachers in Churchill, Manitoba. When the residential school closed, we were asked, "Do you want to go to your home community in Iqaluit where there's a new high school?" I said, "That's not my home community, my home community is Arctic Bay." "But there's a new high school that opened up in Iqaluit. Do you want to go to Ottawa to further your education or do you want to go to Iqaluit, to where there is a new school?" And a lot of us opted to go to Ottawa and continue our education. Because the residential school in Churchill closed, many of the teachers who were there came to Ottawa and they were our counsellors. One of them said to me at one time, "You are very adaptive." I thought about that. I didn't really get what he meant by that. But over time I think I came to understand what he meant. I'm pretty adaptive to where I am. When I was not elected, I just took it on and said, "Okay. Here I am now. Now I will do what I want to do and contribute in the way that I feel I can, where if I have the skills and knowledge and I will share that." I'm pretty much that way, I guess, in situations where I find myself.

KATE GRAHAM: In Canada today, we have all male premiers. Why do you think that is?

EVA AARIAK: That is a good question that men should be asking themselves because women know the answers. There are as many women as there are men who have the skills and knowledge and ability and strength to be in that position. Very much so. I strongly believe that we have enough women out there who can do it but getting there is the question because of all of the obstacles. Sometimes in the small communities where we're from, there's a lack of daycares or support in the home and so on. Sometimes even the voters—women voters and men voters—feel that perhaps the male is more capable. We have the number of women to be in strong leadership. We just have to help them to get there. We just need to help them to get there and understand and support them and perhaps eliminate the barriers that are out there.

KATE GRAHAM: Reflecting back on your time in politics, was it worth it?

EVA AARIAK: Absolutely. Absolutely. I'm very proud of the fact that I was there. There were times when I felt guilty. I felt guilty of not going to my son's hockey game and not watching his practice. Things like that. But at the same time, I think it's important for them to understand where you are and, you know, that you need to let them understand where you are with it and how you feel about it and at the same time, giving them the knowledge of what your role is, what your responsibilities are, and see how they will take it. They are very proud of me, and I love them for that. One of them is quite outspoken and she has been asked many times whether she would be willing to run in certain positions. She's been approached a lot of times now. But she has children and she says to me, "Well, I mean I have that role right now that I need to make sure that, you know, the kids are taken care of." So, in time. But I tell young people who may not feel they are ready, but I know they have that inkling, they have that aptitude, they have that strength in their heart and mind and one day, you know…I just encourage them. When you're ready, do it.

CATHERINE CALLBECK

When driving through rural Prince Edward Island (PEI) to meet with Catherine Callbeck, there are many markers to let you know you're in the right place.

Callbeck Street.

The William Callbeck Centre.

A mural of the Callbeck's tailor shop.

And then, finally, a stately home complete with family portraits inside. You know you have arrived.

Catherine Sophia Callbeck was born on July 25, 1939, in Central Bedeque, Prince Edward Island, into a highly successful family and from a young age became involved in the family business. She completed a Bachelor of Commerce degree from Mount Allison University in 1960, where she was the only woman in the class. This would prove to be the first of many times that Callbeck would be the only woman in the room.

Callbeck entered politics in 1974 when she was elected to the legislative assembly of Prince Edward Island and, three days after the election, was appointed to Cabinet. In 1988, she took the leap into federal politics and was elected as a Liberal member of Parliament for the riding of Malpeque, making her the only woman to hold that seat.

In 1993, she returned to provincial politics and ran successfully for the leadership of the Prince Edward Island Liberal Party.

Callbeck led the party to victory in 1993, making her the first woman in Canada to be elected as premier through a general election. To date, she remains the only woman to have served as premier in Prince Edward Island. She led the province until 1996, when she announced her resignation in July. After her time as premier, she served in the Senate from 1997 to 2014. She currently serves as chancellor for the University of Prince Edward Island.

In Canada's smallest province—a place known for everyone knowing each other—I came to this interview with clear expectations. Although I've never lived on the Island, I consider myself to be part-Islander. My mother grew up in Charlottetown and almost my entire maternal side of the family continues to live there. My parents were both teachers and as soon as school let out each year they would load me and my siblings into our van and we would head for PEI. I spent every summer there and continue to go at least once a year. I'd heard a lot about PEI's first and only female premier. In a province known to be among the most politically engaged in the country, people talk. I knew something of Callbeck's reputation: smart, dedicated, and hardworking. I'd heard about some of her difficult, and sometimes contentious, decisions.

What I found was a woman who in every sense embodied the proud tradition of the institutions she represented on the Island. She welcomed us into her home—the very home she grew up in, almost preserved in time. She showed off the history: black and white photos on the wall, parents and brother, Bill, grandparents, aunts and uncles, and other notable family members; books on the shelf with personal notes from famous Islanders and Canadian political figures.

We sat down over a cup of tea in a drawing room that overlooked the seemingly untouched pastures of another time. This is where I got to see the up-close-and-personal version of what it takes to become the first woman ever elected through a general election to become a first minister in Canada.

"I thought there was no way I was ever going to be in politics because I'm too shy." Catherine Callbeck has served as a member of Prince Edward Island's legislative assembly, a member of Parliament, premier of PEI, and in the Canadian Senate.

KATE GRAHAM: This is such a beautiful setting. Being in someone's home gives you a real sense of the person and who they are, what matters to them.

CATHERINE CALLBECK: It's good to have you in Central Bedeque. It's not a very big place but it's a very important place to me as I grew up in this wonderful village, in this very house. My brother, Bill, and I had a great time growing up here. People were supportive and we knew everyone and were in everybody's house. I attended the two-room school up to Grade 9 and then went into the town of Summerside for high school.

KATE GRAHAM: How many people live in the Bedeque area now?

CATHERINE CALLBECK: Well, we amalgamated with the village of Bedeque so you might have approximately 300 now.

KATE GRAHAM: Well, it's quite a privilege to be sitting here with you today and hear your story. Maybe we can start at the beginning. Tell me where your interest in politics came from.

CATHERINE CALLBECK: Now my interest in politics, well...my family was in business. At that time, it wasn't considered very wise to be actively involved in politics if you're in business, so as a result I didn't hear a lot of political talk in my home. But every Sunday we would go to Summerside, to my grandparents, and my uncle and aunt would be there. My grandfather and my uncle were very much involved in the Liberal Party. And looking back, I know that I was always interested in hearing what they had to say. I guess I was an interested observer. But I really became interested in politics when I went to Mount Allison. On campus they had a very active Liberal Party, and I joined because that's where the action seemed to be....

In my third year, I was asked to run in the model parliament. I said no because I was such a shy, young girl. Friends pushed, and I ran and got elected. Then I ran the next year and again I was successful. It really stimulated my interest in politics. After I graduated from Mount A, I taught for a year and then went to Dalhousie [University], and then to teach at a community college in Saint John, New Brunswick. And it was a civil service job, a teaching position in business administration.

When I came back to Prince Edward Island and became an active partner in the family business, I started getting involved in community events, provincial boards and so on. People would say to me, "Oh, you should be involved in politics," but I would think there was no way I am ever going to be in politics because I am too shy. [laughs] In 1973, we had the PEI Confederation Centennial, and I was asked to chair an event-planning committee of eight area communities. I realized then that if I was ever going to get over my shyness, I had to do it. So, I did. I led the centennial committee, and it was terrific. I had a fabulous committee, and the celebrations were great. The next year, 1974, there was a provincial election. The Liberals asked me to run and so did the Conservatives. I chose to run with the Liberals, and I won.

My election was on Monday, and on Thursday I was in the cabinet with two portfolios. I didn't know too much about government. When I'd told the premier I would run, the cabinet had come up. And I'd said, "I don't want to be in the cabinet. I want to be in business and look after the constituents." The premier had a caucus meeting of all the newly elected members. During that meeting he said, "I'll read out the names of the cabinet." He read them out and there I was, Minister of Health and Social Services. [laughs] I immediately went to his executive assistant, and I said, "I don't want to be in the cabinet." He said, "Well, it's out now and the deputies are meeting the ministers in the room over there." I said, "I want to see the premier." I got to meet the premier in his office and also present was another member of the Legislature who was going to be the next Lieutenant Governor. The member looked at me and said, "Well, if you walk out that door and you don't take this cabinet post, it's game over." The premier called my brother Bill with whom I was in business and we discussed it. Bill said, "Well, you know I'll support you. Do what you want to do." That's how I ended up in the cabinet.

KATE GRAHAM: [laughs] Wow, quite a story! Do you mind if we go back a bit? I'm curious about a couple of key moments. You mentioned when you were first approached to run, you said no a couple of times. What was it that turned that no into a yes?

CATHERINE CALLBECK: Well, I think it was the number of people who came after me to run. I had been in a lot of organizations and causes and so on that I realized the big decisions are not made here in Central Bedeque. They're made in the legislature in Charlottetown and I wanted to be involved in making those decisions. People kept coming after me and saying, "We'll support you." That's what did it. There's a big role for people to play that don't want to get into politics themselves and that is to identify people they think would be good and encourage them to run and support them, work on their campaign. You know, I would never have had twenty-nine years in public life if that hadn't happened.

KATE GRAHAM: At the time of these steps—that first decision to run, when you were in the cabinet—we didn't see a lot of women in those roles at that time. Did your gender factor into how you were thinking about your own career progression?

CATHERINE CALLBECK: I guess when I was on the campaign trail it certainly did. I had men say to me, "I can't vote for you because you're a woman." Some women would say politics is no place for a woman. But I never let that bother me. Maybe because of my background. I was brought up surrounded by strong role models, women role models like my mother, my aunts, the women in the community, the church, and so on. And when I went to Mount Allison in 1956, I was the only woman taking a Bachelor of Commerce. I was the second woman to ever graduate from Mount A in Bachelor of Commerce. Then I taught at community college where I was the only woman on the staff teaching business administration. I came back to Bedeque, and got into the family business here, and the sales reps would all be men. I guess I got comfortable operating among men.

KATE GRAHAM: You mentioned having strong women around you throughout your life. Tell us a little bit more about who they were and how they influenced you.

CATHERINE CALLBECK: My mother certainly was a very strong role model. When my father was living, he ran the business, and she ran the house. After he passed away, she got involved in the business and she had a terrific business head. She would have done extremely well if she had got into it earlier. My aunt Louise—who lived in the other side of the house with my aunt Mildred, and my grandfather—she was a missionary in Japan, probably the first Island woman to ever go around the world on her own. My aunt Mildred had been a teacher out West and came home because her father felt they needed her in the business. Both women really concentrated on young people. They wanted to see youth reach their potential.

KATE GRAHAM: When you were in those environments where you were the only woman, did you ever feel intimidated? Did you experience sexism at the time?

CATHERINE CALLBECK: Look, I wanted to take Bachelor of Commerce. That's what I was set on and that's what I wanted to do. And I don't remember thinking about all this other stuff.

KATE GRAHAM: Okay. Let's talk about your path to becoming the premier. You were an MP at the time. An opportunity opens up with a leadership race. Tell us a bit about your decision to run.

CATHERINE CALLBECK: I certainly did not plan to run to become the premier. I never set out to be a politician. That was not in my thinking at all. Liberal Premier Joe Ghiz announced his resignation in 1996, and my phone started to ring in Ottawa, where I was then an MP in the House of Commons. I told them, "No, I'm not interested at all." But they kept after me. Eventually I decided maybe I can do more for the people as premier than I can as a member of Parliament. I eventually said yes. I found that when I was a member of the PEI legislature and in the provincial cabinet, I was much closer to the people than I was when I was a member of Parliament.

Maybe that's not for everybody, but it was for me. I liked that. I liked constituency work, really helping people, helping solve their problems. I eventually said yes.

KATE GRAHAM: Tell me about the leadership race.

CATHERINE CALLBECK: The leadership race consisted of two men and me. I had a tremendous team, a wonderful team who worked extremely hard for me. They were very supportive and encouraged me all the way. This time, no one said to me, "Politics is no place for women." By this time, the Conservative Party leader was also a woman. That may have been a big factor.

KATE GRAHAM: So, the 1993 election comes along. The two leading parties both have strong female leaders. It ended up being quite a historic election. You were the first woman in Canada to become premier through a general election.

CATHERINE CALLBECK: It certainly was a tremendous experience to go through, to travel from one end of the island to the other and meet with all kinds of people. It's an experience I'll never forget. Every day you were on the road, and you worked from early in the morning till late at night. When the campaign was over, I certainly was excited that I had won and to be the next premier of Prince Edward Island. The victory party is great because I was surrounded by people who supported me and encouraged me and worked for me. They were all happy and it's an opportunity for me to express my gratitude to them. I now have a tremendous responsibility here and will have to deal with all the challenges and the issues. You're down to working hard....

We had a very aggressive agenda. When I went in there was concern about jobs. The unemployment rate was 17 or 18 per cent here. We were running a deficit, the highest deficit ever in the province. There was concern about whether the [fixed] link was going to get built. Electricity rates were the highest in Canada and there were a lot of other issues. Now during my time, we did start and finish the Confederation Bridge. Electricity rates came down. We brought in two balanced budgets—actually one had a surplus. We had electoral reform and municipal reform. And as I say, it was a very aggressive agenda, probably too aggressive. I got to the point that I really was exhausted. I was having trouble with my energy level, which I hadn't experienced before. They couldn't seem to diagnose what the problem was. It was finally diagnosed a year later as rheumatoid arthritis. This disease affects everybody differently, but with me it was the energy. And now, of course, I'm on medication, so it's pretty well under control. At the time, although we were ten points ahead in the party polls, I didn't know how I would make it through another election with my low level of energy. I thought it would be better if someone else took over. I wasn't pushed out. It was my decision to leave and I think it was the only one I could make in that time.

I think one thing you learn is the importance of listening very closely to what people say and try to understand why they think as they do. One of the big things that helped me in the Senate was my time in the legislature. I gained so much knowledge on different areas, the economy, agriculture, health, social services, whatever. It broadened my outlook and I gained a lot of knowledge. When I went into the Senate I learned—as I also did in the legislatures—the importance of committee work, how that can impact public policy. When I went into the Senate, that knowledge was of great help. As you know, the heart and soul of the Senate is committee work, which I really liked, and I worked extremely hard on many issues there.

One thing I would like to add is that when women come to me about running, I tell them, "Look, don't run as a woman candidate. Run as a person. That you're going to look after everybody." I consider it a great honour to have represented people in the provincial legislature, the House of Commons, and the Senate. And I will never forget the people who helped me, supported me, encouraged me, and worked hard on my campaigns, because without those people I would never have had twenty-nine years in public life.

KATE GRAHAM: What do you think of as being your greatest accomplishment?

CATHERINE CALLBECK: I'm most proud of the fixed link, the Confederation Bridge. That took a great deal of time in the first two years I was in the premier's chair, I'm telling you. Joe Ghiz had started it, but then a lot of the people who were supporting it in the federal government were not running again or they sort of were out of the picture. So it took a long while to get that back on track and keep it on track.

KATE GRAHAM: You must feel pretty proud every time you drive across it to know that you made it happen.

CATHERINE CALLBECK: I do. Islanders are so fortunate to have one of the wonders of the world. It led to a great expansion of our economy and, as a result, everybody benefits.

KATE GRAHAM: Today, in 2019, we see very few women make a decision to run for leader and then ultimately become a premier. Only twelve to date have served as a first minister. There are no female premiers today. Why do you think we haven't made more progress?

CATHERINE CALLBECK: Women make up over 50 per cent of the population. That's 50 per cent of the brains. I think it's important to have both men and women taking part and having input in decisions that are going to affect this province and this country. It's easier for men to enter politics than women. It's very difficult for women to find the balance between family and work. That was not a problem for me because I'm not married and don't have children. I think there's a hesitation for women to put themselves out there, whether that comes from their upbringing or way back because it used to be, years and years ago, that men were looked on as the leaders and women sort of as their supporters. But times have changed. I think that we are going to see an awful lot more women get into politics. I can tell you that I have never had more women come and talk to me about wanting to get into politics and run for elected office, whether it's municipal, provincial, or federal. It takes a long while for change.

KATE GRAHAM: What advice do you give women when they come to you?

CATHERINE CALLBECK: Well, I like to first talk to them about whether they've really thought it through and if it is the right time for them to run. It is particularly hard when one has children so I ask if they have a family or young children and if so, have they thought about how politics will affect their family. I am honest in telling them that politics is very demanding. It will take all their time and that I don't know how women with children do it. I ask about how it will impact their career. If they have thought those things through then my advice is simply to get actively involved in their community. Get out there and get into organizations that they care passionately about. I tell them to take an active role so that they will get to know more people and gain name recognition as a hard worker that will represent voters well in the legislature. I also tell them to learn all they can about the issues of the day and if necessary learn public speaking. I advise them to get two or three trustworthy people around them who will tell them the facts rather than just what they want to hear. That's extremely important in politics. I impress upon them the tremendous sense of satisfaction you can get from politics because one is able to help so many people. I share with them that if they want to make a difference then there's no better spot to be in than in government because one has the opportunity to improve the lives of so many people.

CHRISTY CLARK

PREMIER OF BRITISH COLUMBIA
(2011-2017)

Christy Clark holds a few records among leaders in Canada. She is the longest-serving female first minister in Canadian history. She was the second woman in Canada to give birth while serving as a cabinet minister. She is a rare example of someone who left politics and then later made a successful return. And she is the only female premier in Canada to lead her party to a plurality of seats in two consecutive general elections (although the second time didn't exactly work out as planned).

Clark was born and raised in Burnaby, British Columbia. Her first taste of politics came early through her father, a three-time candidate with the BC Liberals. At the time, the centre-right provincial party was in the midst of a nearly four-decade lull. Clark watched her father lose repeatedly with the same party she later led to victory.

Clark studied political science at Simon Fraser University and became involved as a political organizer, serving as the national campaign director for the Young Liberals and working on Parliament Hill. The start to her own political career came in 1996 when she was elected to the legislative assembly as a BC Liberal. Premier Gordon Campbell appointed Clark to Cabinet shortly after and named her as deputy premier. In 2004, Clark announced she was leaving provincial politics to spend more time with her young son. She went on to have a successful media career as host of *The Christy Clark Show*.

In 2010, Clark announced her return to politics with a bid for the leadership of the BC Liberals following Gordon Campbell's retirement. She won and was sworn in as the second female premier of British Columbia. She led the party to victory in 2013, although she herself lost her seat. She was elected shortly after in a by-election and served her government's term as premier. In the 2017 BC election, the party won the most seats but fell one seat short of forming a majority in the legislature. The New Democratic Party (NDP) and the Green Party joined forces in a coalition and defeated Clark's government in a non-confidence vote. Clark resigned soon after.

Christy Clark is someone who has experienced the extreme highs and lows of Canadian politics, but you wouldn't know it to talk to her today. I met Clark at her home in Vancouver, and I'm not sure what I was expecting but walking inside felt decidedly and surprisingly normal. The coffee was brewing. There was sorted mail on the table. Clark's son was busy getting ready for school, with Clark calling out a reminder about the day's cool temperature and an evening commitment as he rushed out the door. Clark was wearing jeans and held a half-drunk green smoothie in one hand as she welcomed us inside.

The normalcy faded away moments later as our team took over her living room with cameras, microphones, and lighting. For most people, this would feel invasive and induce at least some anxiety. Clark, however, seemed even more at ease. She curled up cross-legged on her living room chair as we began our conversation. Her presence effortlessly filled the room with an unmistakable natural charisma and the skill of someone who has spent a career in front of the camera. I remember thinking, 'There it is—star power.'

"If you believe in something, you should stand up for it.
It doesn't matter if you win or lose. You should make your
point." Politician and media personality, Christy Clark,
was the second woman to lead British Columbia as premier.

CHRISTY CLARK: I was the last of four kids—two older brothers, one older sister. It's a great place to be in the birth order. If you talk to birth order theorists, they will tell you that if you're the youngest, you're the one that gets the most attention from your parents—but not the bad attention. On the one hand, your parents have kind of been exhausted by the other kids so they're really not that interested in supervising or disciplining you. But on the other hand, you're the last one and so they just want to lavish you. It was a great place to be, especially since my older brothers completely exhausted my parents—like they had just totally given up. I always say that I didn't really get raised, but I was loved. The one thing that we do know about healthy kids and attachment is that it's not how many orders your parents are giving you and whether or not they're making you eat your peas. It's whether or not they love you. That's it, that's all. I got lots of love. It was an awesome place to begin....

My dad was a schoolteacher and an iconoclast. He was a BC Liberal, which was very unusual in those days because, remember, the Social Credit Party was the coalition party of liberals and conservatives, and everybody was trying to keep the NDP out of government at all costs. My dad decided that he was going to be a BC Liberal and he ran in 1966, 1969, and in 1975. We used to have to door-knock for him as little kids and we were all folding brochures. He would get 4 per cent or 5 per cent of the vote or something. And then we would have these political conversations around the table. That was what I grew up with. You know, some people don't talk religion and politics? We talked religion and politics! More politics. It was lively.

KATE GRAHAM: In those early days, when you were out door-knocking and doing pamphlets and so on, did you ever think that someday you would run?

CHRISTY CLARK: No. I never thought about that. [pause] I didn't ever think about politics as being something that you could be successful at. [laughs] My dad was never successful. I just thought it was something that you did because you cared about things, and you had your opinions and you wanted to do good things. Getting elected wasn't really the point—at least, I must have decided it wasn't the point because my dad never got elected and nobody was ever disappointed that he didn't get elected because no one expected he would. He was trying to make a point. I guess that was the lesson that I learned from it: if you believe in something, you should stand up for it. It doesn't matter if you win or lose. You should make your point.

KATE GRAHAM: What were those election nights like when you were a kid? Your dad wasn't successful. You weren't really expecting him to be. Was it a celebration? What do you remember about those nights?

CHRISTY CLARK: Well, I don't really…. I mean, I was one in 1966, right?

KATE GRAHAM: [laughs] That's a very early start.

CHRISTY CLARK: I do remember 1975 a little bit better because I was ten. The Social Credit came back and got rid of the NDP government and my dad lost, of course. I think he did the worst in that election because the anti-NDP vote was really strong and there just wasn't space for a third-party vote. So, I just remember a lot of drinking. [laughs]

KATE GRAHAM: Okay. Walk me through how those experiences then led to the moment where you decided that you were going to run as a candidate yourself for the first time.

CHRISTY CLARK: I went through high school, and I was always interested in politics. I was the only kid who was interested in politics at school and, you know, people would make fun of me for it—but not in a terrible way, right? I was always arguing with everybody about everything, and I was winning because nobody knew anything about politics. They were fifteen! So, I went to university. Lots of people drop out their first year because they're depressed. They go from high school, having people know who you are and teachers paying attention to you, to the university, where you really realize it's all on you and nobody cares. I was kind of wandering around university and I thought, 'You know, I'm going to join the Young Liberals club and I'm going to have some friends.' That's what I did....

I got involved in youth politics. I went from that to getting a job working for [former BC Liberal Party leader] Gordon Wilson's caucus. I met one of my lifelong best friends in that process, Mike McDonald, who became my chief of staff and my campaign director. He's basically busted his back working to get me elected over the years. Mike and I drove around the province in one of the MLA's [member of the legislative assembly's] old vans, racking up speeding tickets that the other guy had to pay for, trying to find candidates to run for Gordon Wilson. That was our whole goal. But we were twenty-two and completely not credible....

But we knew Gordon Wilson could be credible. We had to get him into the provincial debate. CBC or somebody had set the thing, [saying,] "Look you have to have candidates in every riding if you want to be in the debate." So, we said, "Okay, we're going to go find candidates." We weren't credible, but neither were any of the people we were trying to persuade to be candidates. There was a guy who was starting a mustard factory in Quesnel and some guy named Rocky who we never ended up meeting. He could have been phoning us from jail. [laughs] We didn't know. We would sit in the hot tubs with people and say, "Okay, so do you want to run?" And they would go, "No." And we'd say, "Okay, what about your wife?" And they would shout across the room, "Hey honey, you want to run?" And she'd say, "No, I'm not running, you run." And then we'd go, "Okay. Here's what we're gonna do. You and me and your wife are going to get your neighbour to run." We got almost a full slate of candidates and we got him into the debate. That was what we did. But I never thought of myself as being a candidate. That never occurred to me.

KATE GRAHAM: Wait, all of these conversations, sitting in hot tubs and asking people to run...it never dawned on you that you should run?

CHRISTY CLARK: Never.

KATE GRAHAM: A bright, university-educated young woman...

CHRISTY CLARK: No.

KATE GRAHAM: ...let alone someone who would become...

CHRISTY CLARK: Nope.

KATE GRAHAM: ...the future premier?

CHRISTY CLARK: I know. It's funny because my friends from high school look back and say, "We always knew you'd be premier." And I would say, "How did you know that, and I didn't?" But the thing is, they didn't know, right? It's all hindsight; you knit things back together. I never thought about running for office. It was a weird thing that I actually ended up doing it....

I went to work on the National Youth Campaign for Chrétien in the 1993 election and then worked in Ottawa for Doug Young when he was minister of transportation. I was doing that when Gordon Campbell became the leader [in BC]. Mike McDonald—the hot tub guy, the speeding ticket guy—he ran Gordon Campbell's campaign for leader. And then my brother Bruce ran into Gordon Campbell himself in an airport lounge. He said, "You know, you should get my sister to run." Gordon was really looking for women candidates at the time and he couldn't find any candidates, really, in Burnaby, which is where we grew up, and so Gordon just phoned me and said, "Look, I think you should run." And I thought, 'Oh, that's weird.' I talked to my then–partner-boyfriend—later my husband, now my ex-husband—about it and he said, "Yeah, why not? Let's move back to BC." So, I did it....

The thing is, I have a strong appetite for risk. I don't mind taking risks at all. My view of life is that opportunities are raining down around us all the time for everybody. Some people have fewer opportunities, no question about it, because their circumstances haven't put them in a spot that's really rainy. But it's always there. We just have to look around and figure out which opportunities you want to grab. A lot of people decide they just don't want to grab those opportunities because they feel it might be risky. But I don't mind risk. So, I thought, 'Why not? What have I got to lose? I could lose, I guess! And then what would I do after that? Well, I'll figure it out.' [laughs]

That's kind of been the story of my life. I think that is sort of a youngest child thing, right, which is kind of a "Okay I'll figure it out." The oldest kids, there's all this pressure and they've got to perform and mum and dad are really thinking, "Here's your plan. You've got to do this." I'm probably like that with my own son because I only have one. But by the time that came along with me, they just sort of said, "You figure it out." I don't think I'm making my parents sound really good. [laughs] But they were awesome.

KATE GRAHAM: Okay. You make this step. You've been around politics a long time but now you're the candidate, and then you're the member.

CHRISTY CLARK: Yes.

KATE GRAHAM: Thinking about that early time you emerged as a political figure, what was the experience like? Did anything surprise you?

CHRISTY CLARK: I was terrible at it. I didn't expect to be so bad at it. [laughs]

KATE GRAHAM: What?

CHRISTY CLARK: I know. Being a politician's like being a carpenter. You learn. You get better at it.

KATE GRAHAM: What were you not good at?

CHRISTY CLARK: I wasn't good at public speaking. I wasn't good at debating. I didn't look good on TV. I didn't know how to dress. I wasn't good at persuading people to vote for me. I wasn't good at anything. I mean, I was a hardworking candidate, no question.

I had some great people around me who were helping me, including my now-ex-husband who gave me fantastic advice. We just were grinding, really working hard. Mine was the only campaign that won between Boundary Road, which is the edge of Vancouver, and gosh, almost Abbotsford? The NDP swept the suburbs in every riding except for mine because we just worked harder. We outworked them. But I was not a good candidate. And then I get elected and I go into the legislature, and I was terrible. [laughs] Every once in a while, I pull out the DVD video of my nomination speech. I show it to Hamish, my son, just so he can laugh at me because it's so bad and so funny. He looks and he's like, "Is that even you? How could you have been so unbelievably awful?" I was. But I learned and I got better.

KATE GRAHAM: Do you feel like being a woman factored into how you perceived yourself?

CHRISTY CLARK: You know, it's interesting. My previous work experience had kind of been as a political helper, right? I'd done some business, a little consulting and things like that, but mostly I had been a political staffer. I was at a lower end of that, too; I wasn't really competing for the top jobs because I was young. I was twenty-nine when I got nominated. I didn't really feel sexism the same way. But then when I was in the field with the big players, people who are Queen's Counsel and lawyers and mayors and doctors—people who were sixty, seventy years old, lots of life experience—I banged up against that for the first time and realized that being a woman is not an asset in a lot of ways. People always underestimate women. Sometimes it's good to be underestimated. But the problem with the way we think about women is that we have low expectations, people assume we're not going to perform. There's a built-in bias that men and women have of women, that we're just not capable of performing to a higher level. For men, because expectations are higher, they are able to meet a higher level. It's that thing where you're sitting around the table—and every single woman tells this story no matter what world she's been in—where you say something and then nobody says anything. The guy next to you says the same thing. "Oh, James, that is such a great point!" And the woman is inevitably saying, "I just told you that!" [laughs]

When I look back, I realize it's why college students in the United States didn't care about voting for Hillary Clinton. They haven't hit that yet. They haven't had that happen to them yet. But it's when you get out there and you're in your thirties and forties that you really realize that, as one researcher put it, it's not a glass ceiling. It's not *boom*—you hit something, and it's a problem. You look back and you realize it's a labyrinth and you've been trying to overcome all these obstacles along the way. Every one of those obstacles as a woman has slowed you down in your ascent. It's not like women are allowed to get so high and then *boom*, you're done. It's all along the way you are trying to overcome sexism. It's not only true for women in politics; it's just more visible for us, I think.

KATE GRAHAM: Roll the clock forward. You had some significant political accomplishments. You'd served as a cabinet minister, then took some time away to focus on family. Walk me through the decision to throw your hat in the ring to become the leader of the party. Very few women in the entire history of our country have been bold enough to make that choice. What led you to say, "Okay I'm going to run for leader?"

CHRISTY CLARK: Well, there were a lot of people in the race, and it didn't seem like any of them had a chance of winning. I was in broadcasting. I thought I had a pretty good career trajectory. I was doing well financially. It was a lot to leave behind, but I'd worked so hard and devoted so much of my life to supporting the BC Liberals. I thought of my dad—when nobody else was going to run...he did it. He set that example for me, and I felt like I should set that example for my son. And I thought it was a chance to really make a difference....

I knew that it was going to be really tough. It was a suicide mission at the time. We were way back in the polls. Our party was a disaster. Our caucus had just had a massive revolt. None of them really loved me—or they were ambivalent toward me. There was no reason to think we would win the next election. We had no money. You know, it was terrible. Nobody good wanted to do it. [laughs]

KATE GRAHAM: If it had been different circumstances, do you think you would have run? If the party was doing well and there were lots of great candidates in the race, would you have stepped forward?

CHRISTY CLARK: Maybe? It depends who the candidates were. I mean it's an impossible question to answer, Kate, because there were some really outstanding candidates who could have stepped in. Carole Taylor could have stepped in, but she decided not to. The reason none of the candidates in the race were really dead ringers for the win was because the party was so unpopular. I had taken a whole bunch of time out, so I was kind of an outsider candidate. It's an impossible question to answer—but once again, opportunities present themselves to you sometimes only once. My view is you should take them.

KATE GRAHAM: Just...take them? [laughs]

CHRISTY CLARK: Why not? All you can do is lose and then you go do something else.

KATE GRAHAM: But you didn't lose. You won.

CHRISTY CLARK: Yeah. [laughs] Those first few years were really hard. That was the hardest thing I've ever done from an emotional perspective. It was very hard for me to get my message across, especially on my fiscal credentials. I had a very strong view that we needed to balance the budget. I promised to constrain the growth in spending on healthcare, which was the fastest-growing area of the budget. We had a huge deficit. All of my opponents said, "She doesn't understand what she's talking about. She doesn't understand." It was really hard for me to prove that I did understand how money worked. I did understand the budget. And I did understand that to balance the budget you need to constrain government growth and government spending in the fastest-growing areas of government spending. And you need a target to do that. When my opponents said, "She just doesn't understand," the media kind of took that as gospel. That was the funny part. Well, I just explained it. But when my opponents, who were all men, said that it became "the facts." That I wasn't good at budgeting. You know, because girls aren't good at math, right?

KATE GRAHAM: Did anybody call that out?

CHRISTY CLARK: No. Throughout my career there was almost no comment about the sexist treatment of me. The thing about sexism is that it works. It works. What people forget is, left or right, parties want to win. And many parties will use whatever means they have at their disposal to win. And if that means deploying sexist messages and sexist language because it works, they will do it....

You can't do anything about it. The minute you say, "Hey that was sexist," it's, "Oh look, she's just whining, isn't she?" Women are very careful about calling out sexism. Kathleen Wynne was very careful about calling out homophobic comments for the same reason, because you're so lucky to have the job. It's a privilege to do it.

KATE GRAHAM: How do you think sexism shaped your tenure as premier?

CHRISTY CLARK: I think what happened with me was really that classic dilemma that women face between being liked and being tough. You don't get to be both; men do. You can like a tough guy, but people don't like tough women—and people don't think women are tough enough if they like them. So, you're either one or the other or you're somewhere in between. Heaven forbid you're somewhere in between! I started out as likeable. I'd been in people's homes a lot because I was on the radio, and then I became tough. And, people would say, "I don't like her. I really don't like her." People would complain about my policy decisions if they didn't like them: "Welfare rates aren't high enough." Okay, fair enough, that's a legitimate concern. We think the carbon tax should be higher or lower or whatever. But I remember with Kathleen, people wouldn't even say what they were mad at her about. They would just say, "We don't like her." People don't do that with men. People just don't do it. They did with me, though, too. That's what we would see in focus groups. "I don't know what it is about her, I just don't like her. I don't like looking at her face or hearing her voice. I don't like her."

KATE GRAHAM: So, what's underneath that? Unpack that for me.

CHRISTY CLARK: I don't really care that much about what… well, I shouldn't say I don't really care. It's not the way to put it. I care a lot about what people I respect think about me. I respect them and their opinions matter to me. If they are negative, I can take those on board and I can use them to become a better person. But people who don't know me? Nah. It's not really something I can control because if it's coming from a place of, "I just I don't know what it is." Well, what do you do with that? It's sexism, right? We don't think about male leaders that way.

KATE GRAHAM: It's a really common thing, unfortunately, that we're hearing through a number of these interviews. The likability factor for women is so important and so fleeting. And when it's gone, it's politically catastrophic.

CHRISTY CLARK: Yeah, it's a real problem. There are other things, too, like ambition. It's a dirty word for women and it's a compliment for men. I mean there is a well-known columnist in BC I remember from when I first started running for leader. His comment was, "Oh she's so ambitious." And the context made it clear that it wasn't a compliment. But, don't you want your kids to be ambitious? I mean, ambition is a good thing! And I don't know how you succeed in a world like politics—which is so rough-and-tumble and incredibly competitive—without seeming like you're ambitious. It's not structured to be a game women can win.

KATE GRAHAM: What does that say about us as Canadians when we judge male and female leaders so differently? And for women, if the standard is something unattainable—as you said to be simultaneously nice and tough and likable and so on—what does that say about us?

CHRISTY CLARK: I think it tells us that we live in a sexist society. We take on those sexist biases unconsciously. It's not like men are sexist and women are not. Women are sexist, too. Women take on these biases. We grow up with it. We are surrounded by it. I don't have a great solution to this except we need to keep working and elect a lot more women. We need to get used to women being in political roles. It's the only thing that's going to change it.

You know, the research shows that women are extremely competitive with other women, just as men are extremely competitive with other men. But women are less likely to compete when it comes to men. So, we compete with women and when we get into a man's world, we defer. You know, "I was happy to be a part of a much larger team that made such a difference," and, "I just really feel like credit is due to the entire team." But then there's Johnny over there going, "Yep. It was me. It was awesome, and it was me." [laughs]

We do judge women. Quite harshly. We've grown up in a world where all of our competitive instinct is focused on other women. We need more women around the table, and once we get there, we have to get past competing against each other.

I find amongst women who've been successful—you know, the women who head up the big accounting firms or big law firms, or the women who have run big companies, or women in politics—they've been through those wars, and they got there somehow. There is a band of sisters when you get there and that was for sure true of my cabinet. It was half women most of the time and I really felt a sisterhood with them. We'd all been punched in the nose enough through all the sexism we'd endured in getting there. I was really blessed with my cabinet. One of them was a multi-medalist—gold medalist—Paralympic athlete. She's just an unbelievable competitor but a real team player. I had these incredible women in my cabinet who didn't really fight to try and get credit. That's the one thing [laughs] about having women on your team. They just work, they get their noses down, let other people take the credit if that's necessary. It was a great group. Oh. Here I am deferring! [laughs]

KATE GRAHAM: [laughs] You know the phrase, the higher you rise the further you fall. You've had a lot of ups and downs in your career. But this last election—I mean, the entire country was watching, and it was a bizarre set of circumstances. Do you think gender is a part of that campaign or what happened?

CHRISTY CLARK: I do. One of the common archetypes for women is the witch. She's evil. She's corrupt. It was a very easy label to put on Hillary Clinton. "Crooked Hillary." It works for women—crooked. It works because it plays into that archetype. And the NDP really used that in this case. This campaign was 'this woman is a crook.' She's crooked, she's dishonest, she's a cheating, corrupt woman. It goes back to all these myths about women. We are the betrayers. We are the cheaters. We are the adulteresses. We are the witches. All of those archetypes are boiled down in the way people talk about women in politics. Kathleen Wynne got it. Alison Redford got it. I got it. Hillary Clinton got it. It's not entirely unique to women, but it sticks with women. There was just a lot of talk about how I dressed and who I was dating and was I fat or thin or whatever. I said earlier, political parties want to win. They will do anything to win. They're not high-minded or principled, because sexism and sexist labels work. And corrupt, cheating sticks with women better than it does with men. They use that a lot. And it really did stick in a lot of ways....

So, we won the election. We got the most seats. We got the most votes. The NDP and the Greens were trying to cobble together enough seats to defeat the government. Our job—my job—under the Constitution was to form a government because we had the most seats and the most votes. And then if we couldn't, we had to demonstrate that by introducing a throne speech and having it be defeated in the house. That was my job. So, I spent a month trying to get a throne speech that would pass and then be able to govern, one seat short of a majority. We didn't get there. The lieutenant governor had to decide whether or not she would call an election or whether she was going to appoint a new government. When I met with her about it, it was obvious to me that she'd made her decision. I left that meeting and said to my staff, "I'm pretty sure she's going to call on the NDP." She had privately told the NDP that earlier in the day. They knew they were going to form the government, we think—the morning of that day—but when I met with her, it was like was a eureka moment. We were the last ones to know....

But you don't know until it's done. Politics is a weird thing. It's a painful process and getting to the end of it was—that part of it was a relief. I felt so badly, though, that I didn't carry the whole team across the line. Because one thing I know about politics is when you're the leader, it's all on your shoulders. It's not, "Oh gee, we had a great team." You either win it for everybody or you lose it for everybody. And we lost it. I mean we won the election, but we lost the government. I take full responsibility for that and I feel terrible about that because we had the province on such a good track, and I felt so good about all the jobs we were creating and all the families that were supported. I felt badly because, I'd taken on a job and I'd failed at delivering the one thing a leader has to do: win an election. Well, [laughs] it turns out you have to do two things: You have to win an election and you have to hold on to the government.

In the days after, it took me a little while to get used to not being phenomenally busy all the time. I look back at it now and I'm sorry that we're not in government. But I'm feeling great about my new life. I mean, I'm fifty-three years old. My son is about to go off to university. I have a whole great life ahead of me and a brand-new chapter in my life that I don't have to share with the public and the media. It's not going to be as fulfilling. It's not going to be as meaningful. Being premier was absolutely a peak experience. I'll never do anything as meaningful and fulfilling as that again. But I did it and I'm one of the few who did. And I feel like I made a big difference. So, you know, now it's somebody else's turn. I think we all have that obligation. And I feel confident that I have fulfilled my obligation. So now I'm going to go have a good life.

KATE GRAHAM: Even with all the highs and lows, if you could go back and do the whole thing again, would you?

CHRISTY CLARK: Absolutely. There are things that I would have approached differently and there are a lot of lessons. But that's life, isn't it? I mean, I would have been a better parent probably if I'd known all these things when Hamish was seven months old that I know when he's seventeen years old. I would have been a better daughter. You learn as you go along....

We [need to] get more women elected. That's really the most important thing. We [need to] support more women in becoming the heads of big organizations in the country, in corporate Canada. And we [need to] support great organizations in Canada that are helping women. We should be measuring how many women are on boards. I think we also have to start calling out the media and politicians for implicitly sexist and misogynist language and labels. But what politician is going to say to a journalist, "You know, that was a really sexist question." Especially since half the time it's women asking those questions. There have to be people calling them out on it and it is not happening in Canada right now....

I would also say that political parties have been remarkable in just how badly they've failed in helping women get elected. What political parties do is say that half the candidates will be women. Great. But...the women will be running in ridings where nobody is going to win. Right? And the really tough competitions are for nominations in the ridings where you're most likely to win. Political parties need to do a better job supporting women through those nominations. I'm a believer that political parties should be appointing women if that's what it takes. We should be cancelling nominations if that's what it takes. I really think that there must be more dramatic action taken to make sure that women get elected.

KATE GRAHAM: What advice would you have for women who are thinking about running for politics, or maybe who are thinking about taking that big step and running for a leadership position?

CHRISTY CLARK: Women—I'm talking to you now—I know you think you're a fraud. I know you think you don't know the answers to all the questions. I know you think you don't have any time to do this and now is just not the moment. And you know how I know that? Because every single woman says that whenever I've asked her to run. It is an absolutely universal thing. And then you go, and you ask men to run, and they go, "I can't believe it took you so long to think of me. I really can't." That's the first thing the men say. "It's so obvious. I'd be a great candidate." And he's not sitting there thinking, "Oh, gee, I don't know the platform. What if I get asked a question I don't know the answer to? I might look like an idiot." As women, we're raised in this world where we're constantly told we're not competent. There's a thousand different little ways that society tells us we're not competent. You're not good enough. We grow up with that. So then, our answer is that we have to be perfect because the minute we make a mistake and we say something stupid, we're going to be proven to be frauds. We're going to prove that we're not competent. And men just don't live with that kind of pressure. That's the first thing. Women, we have just got to get over ourselves and say, "You know what? I don't have to know the answer to everything. And, you know what? I'm going to bullshit this one just like the guys do all the time...."

I mean, we have so much on our shoulders. Kids. Husbands who are sometimes like an extra kid. The dog lost his ability to control his own bowels and you've got to clean it up. Mom's got dementia. Who's looking after all that stuff? The woman. Many women who are at an age with family responsibilities will say, "It's just not the right time for me." But it is never, ever, the right time to run for politics. It is never going to be the right time. There's always a reason not to do it. And women always find that reason and men never do....

Women like me have to work even harder to get more women to run. We can't sit around thinking the world's going to change. We've all got to step up and decide we want to do it. I will never do anything as fulfilling and as hard as what I did in politics. But it made me a better person. I think I made the province a better place. I think it made my son a better person watching me go through all that—because it was really difficult. If, at the end of our lives, we want to look back and have been the best possible person we could be, we have to do really hard things. So, I think we have to keep up the push. We're going to have to keep fighting for it. We're going to have to recognize our own internal biases. We're going to have to constantly be pushing and getting women to run for office and then supporting and promoting and mentoring women once they get there. There's just, there's no end to it. Equality is not something that happens. Equality is something you fight for.

CAROLINE COCHRANE

PREMIER OF NORTHWEST TERRITORIES
(2019 TO THE PRESENT)

When the *No Second Chances* project concluded in June 2019, there were no female first ministers in Canada. This changed just a few months later—in October, Caroline Cochrane was elected premier of the Northwest Territories (NWT).[5]

Roll the clock forward two years to the summer of 2021, Cochrane still sits as the lone woman on the Council of the Federation, and the world has changed. The first two years of Cochrane's term included a historic convergence of crises: a global pandemic, complete with a catastrophic loss of life and one of the most significant economic contractions in Canadian history that is taking women's participation in the workforce back three decades; a concerning rise in mental health and addictions struggles, including deaths from opioids; climate change-induced fires and natural disasters, including the first mass casualty event in Canada related to the climate crisis; a period marked by long-needed reckonings over racial injustices and oppression, including hundreds of thousands protesting in Black Lives Matter marches in cities around the world as well as calls for reconciliation with the discovery of more than a thousand unmarked graves of Indigenous children.

....

[5] The fourteenth, Premier Heather Stefanson of Manitoba, was sworn into office in November 2021, bringing the number of women in first minister positions in Canada at the time up to two.

In other words, to say that Cochrane was governing at a difficult time would be an understatement.

I reached out to Cochrane as this book was being prepared. She agreed to an interview, and we met via Zoom call (as was customary in this pandemic era). She called in from her office in the Northwest Territories—and even through the distance of space and time, her inspiring story made me catch my breath.

Cochrane was born in Flin Flon, Manitoba, in 1960. She moved to Yellowknife at the age of three. After a difficult childhood, she left home and lived as a homeless youth at the age of thirteen. This experience proved to have a defining influence on the life and career that followed, leading her to pursue an education in social work, run a women's shelter, and eventually, run for political office. During our interview, she spoke about her swearing-in ceremony where, rather than inviting dignitaries or family, she invited a group of homeless women to join her in the legislature. A framed photo of the group was one of the few objects on her desk in the premier's office, and she proudly showed me the smiling faces of the group on this important day. Far from the traditional formal event photo with people neatly lined up with folded hands and tight smiles, this group photo was decidedly rambunctious: it showed a group of women embracing and cheering, arms and legs moving in every direction.

Cochrane's story is unusual for a premier, characterized by her being a total outsider to politics. She spoke about not knowing what a member of the legislative assembly (MLA) was or who served as premier when she first decided to run. She shared frank (and at points, angering) stories about how alone she is among the other premiers. She expressed her clear post-COVID policy agenda—housing and mental health—and that she was quite prepared to challenge and push leaders across Canada toward action.

When the interview ended, I sat quietly for some time. She left me inspired, motivated, and deeply grateful to Premier Cochrane for being in these spaces with the critical perspectives she brings. As Canada slowly emerges from a time marked by layers of crises, we are collectively grappling with finding our "new normal" and "building back better." The silver lining of chaos and disruption seems to be a real, meaningful appetite for change and progress. Somehow it feels even more urgent today than it did in 2019 that we see more leaders like Cochrane rise to and hold power if we are to address the inequities, injustices, and most pressing challenges we face. Greater diversity among our most senior leaders must be a part of the path forward. It will require us to support leaders who do not fit the conventional mould, but instead bring the very perspectives and backgrounds that have been missing from the table for so long. Perhaps this will be *our* second chance.

"Work with your team, and it's okay not to know everything." Caroline Cochrane was sworn into the Northwest Territories legislative assembly accompanied by women residents of the shelter where she had worked. In her second term, she was elected premier.

CAROLINE COCHRANE: I'm a diamond driller's daughter from the Northwest Territories. I'm a Métis woman. My mother is Métis from Petal Prairie in Alberta. My father is from here. He came to the Northwest Territories with my mom almost sixty years ago because he was a diamond driller. Life was tough. The people in the North worked hard—and they played hard. That came into my family life as well. There was a lot of alcoholism and family violence. I left home when I was thirteen. I didn't even graduate from high school. I struggled through life. I had two children and, on the birth of my second child, I realized that my life wasn't going anywhere. My children's father had gotten into drugs. We'd separated and I was a single mom. I decided that I needed to do something for myself. My father had raised me. He was very traditional, and he said a woman's place was in the home. "All you need to do is be a good wife. And if you are a good wife, you will have a happy life." Well, I tried that a few times and it never worked for me. I realized that instead of a man making me happy, I needed to make myself happy and provide for my children. So, I went to university....

I got a degree in social work, and I moved from there. I spent twenty years working in the non-profit sector—and then my partner got really tired of hearing me complain about the government and not doing anything. One day he came home and said, "Honestly, I'm sick of hearing you talk about this. If you're going to keep talking about it, do something about it." I didn't really know what that meant at first. He said, "You know, you could be an MLA. You're smart enough." I didn't even know what an MLA was. I knew nothing about politics. I didn't know who our premier was. But he opened that door for me. We have a very good relationship, but I needed somebody to push me. And he said, "You can do it."

There was a workshop for women thinking about going into politics. I took it to learn basic skills, and I thought, 'Yeah, I can do this.' I took that to heart. I ran. I campaigned. I won. Now this is my second time. The first time, I became a minister. I did it again and this time I ran and became the premier. So, I can do it. You can do it. We can do it.

KATE GRAHAM: Wow. Thank you. I'm wondering if you can take me back a bit. You left home at thirteen having already been through so much. I gather you never would've imagined then that you would become the premier one day.

CAROLINE COCHRANE: No, no. I never thought I would even live to this age. My life was pretty rough. I was involved in a lot of things that I wouldn't want to see my children or other people dealing with. I always thought that politics was for people who had lots of money, lots of connections, and lots of education—but that's not true. It actually doesn't matter if you have lots of money or an education. It helps, but education isn't just formal education. There are life experiences that also bring a form of education. As long as your heart is in the right place and you genuinely care about people, you don't have to have all of the knowledge. You will work with your team. That's why you have one. There's nobody out there in the world who has all the answers. But as a team, you will make the best decisions. That's something I hold dear to me: work with your team, and it's okay not to know everything.

KATE GRAHAM: I'd like to hear more about your decision to run for office. You talked about needing that push. Walk me through what it took to move from hearing that comment to going to file your papers for the first time.

CAROLINE COCHRANE: My partner gave me the little push I needed. He gave me the opportunity I was looking for: "Yes, you can do this. Go ahead and try." When I took the campaign school, I was really focused on learning skills I needed—to build a team, to write promotional materials, to fundraise. It's really tough for women to ask for money. I didn't have resources. I maxed out my Visa when I ran, actually, because I was too shy to ask for money. I never made that mistake a second time, though! And then I had to develop a platform. It's really easy to say, "I want to be in politics. I want change." But what change do you want and why do you want that? Those were the hands-on skills they gave me in the campaign school. The first thing was I needed a team. I'm not used to asking for help. I came from a tough life. I've learned that when you ask for help, it comes with obligations. As a woman, I never wanted those obligations because some of them weren't nice. So, I've always been firmly independent. Asking for help and finding a team was a huge struggle for me. I ran a non-profit organization and, amazingly, my board became my team. The board of directors for the Women's Society here in Yellowknife had so much confidence in their executive director that they became my team members. That was incredible. It was women supporting women and they not only gave me the confidence to do it, they kept me going. When you go door to door, sometimes people can be cruel. "Who are you? What do you think? Why do you deserve to be in politics? We don't want women in leadership. We don't want you there." Many times, I thought about stepping back and taking "my rightful place" in society and running the homeless shelter—because I could do that—but it was the women behind me saying "we believe in you" that kept me going and kept me knocking on those doors and taking the beatings....

When I was elected, my family wasn't able to come to the swearing-in ceremony—although my mom did show up at the last minute as a surprise. Instead, it was the women from the homeless shelter who came to the ceremony. Everybody else had mothers, fathers, all these well-to-do people, people known in the community, standing beside them for the swearing-in. I had homeless women. Here's a picture of that day. These women from the homeless shelter had never set foot in the legislative assembly and I brought them into the chamber with me that day. It was really powerful. I haven't been working directly with them now for the last six years, but they don't forget me. I was shopping the other day and one of them saw me on the street and screamed out, "Caroline, my politician!" People often judge homeless people, but they are some of the most humble people in the world. They've just been hurt.

KATE GRAHAM: So true—and I suspect you understand that in a way that few political leaders do. So now you're elected for the first time. Did you face any barriers as a woman in your new role as an MLA?

CAROLINE COCHRANE: Absolutely. In the Northwest Territories, we're kind of isolated in some ways. It takes a certain person to come to the Northwest Territories. It's a hard life. It's cold. It's forty below. Life is tough. Prices are expensive. So, it takes a hardy person to come here and decide to set roots here, and most people assume that being hardy is a man's job, that it's not so much a woman's job. Women just come to make sure they're fed and have a clean bed to sleep in, I guess. When I first got elected, I had one MLA who ran against me and that felt I "took his seat." For three months or so before Covid hit, I had nothing but challenges in the house [legislature]. Every time I turned around, there were people trying to find ways to take me out. They'd say, "See? We were right. Women can't lead." I had people from the very beginning on social media saying that the sky was going to fall, that the economy was going to go to hell, everything was going to fall apart. Well, you know what? The sky never fell. The economy is stronger than many others as we come through Covid. We never had to close everything. We opened up slowly. We didn't bounce back and forth as other jurisdictions did. We've done a great job—and it's shown that a women can do this job.

KATE GRAHAM: I'm curious about what it's been like to lead with a consensus government model during this time. The Northwest Territories are one of just two jurisdictions in the country with this model. Do you think that this model, as we often hear, provides a more welcoming environment for women to lead, including during a crisis?

CAROLINE COCHRANE: I think that any kind of political system has its challenges and its strengths. Sometimes I hear that people are jealous of the consensus government because we don't have to have political parties. We're all independent and we work on what we really believe is the right thing. That is a strength of consensus. What people fail to realize is consensus government means that I don't have the luxury of picking my ministers. I have to work with whoever is elected to be a minister yet I'm responsible for making sure that they do their work. That makes it very difficult. When I was the executive director of the homeless shelter, I got to pick my staff. I got to pick my management team. I don't get that in politics, and in a consensus system you have to learn to work with the skills and weaknesses of all people. And that takes some strategy. The other thing with consensus government—and that I think women are better at—is building consensus to get something through the house. We're always a minority government, so we spend a lot of time working with regular members. When you work together as a team, you do make better decisions.

KATE GRAHAM: Can you walk me through how you made the decision to seek the premiership?

CAROLINE COCHRANE: Sometimes the worst enemy for women is our own self-doubt. When I finished the last term of government, I was considering running for this assembly again. I never thought about being premier. I had actually given my vote to another minister who was going to run. They had been tailoring this male minister for over a year, and I just made the assumption he was going to be premier. I asked him, "If you become premier and I vote for you, will you give me the housing portfolio back?" because I came from homelessness and my heart was in homelessness. Ironically, he never got elected as an MLA. So then, we all were in the house and there was just myself and one other member who had any experience in Cabinet. So, at that point, it was like…. Okay, it's now or never. And again, I had to push myself and say, "You do deserve to be there. Why would you not?" Because women are great at second-guessing themselves and I did that. It was a matter of challenging my own belief system. Once I got over that and said, "Yes, you do deserve to be there." Win or lose, it didn't matter at that point. I put my hand up and decided to run for premier. And here I sit today.

KATE GRAHAM: You are the second female premier in the Northwest Territories, after Nellie Cournoyea. Do you think being the second made an easier path for you?

CAROLINE COCHRANE: I think it's a yes and a no. Professionally, no, it never made much difference because Nellie was elected thirty years ago. So, for many years, people were used to seeing men lead. Not only was there no woman premier, there were no women ministers, and at times no women MLAs. We hadn't even broken one or two. I think two of nineteen was our maximum then in history. Now, I'm excited to share that we just had another woman elected. A male MLA stepped down to run for grand chief and we just had an election for his seat yesterday. And we have another woman—that makes us ten of the nineteen. My staff is just doing the background research now, but I think we're the first government in history to actually have the majority of women in leadership....

But for me, personally, Nellie was incredible. Nellie gave me that self-esteem to say that, yes, women can do it. At some point people voted for a woman to be there. Knowing that she went through this process as well gave me the strength to carry on professionally or personally to say that I have a shot at this. So, I think role-modeling is critical. I'm really proud of having ten women now, a majority of the assembly, because this opens the way for other women. It might take thirty years, you know, like Nellie was for me, but hopefully not. Hopefully I will see women in the assembly forever now. Even though it was thirty years ago, it still made an impression on me.

KATE GRAHAM: Let's talk about your time as premier. What an exceptionally difficult time to be in this role.

CAROLINE COCHRANE: It's been a challenge, for sure. It's been really difficult. When Covid first began, we didn't know if we were going to live or die—and it really shows who the true leaders are. Just like everybody else, at the beginning I also thought, 'What do I do with my family? Do I grab everyone and go live in the bush?' Of course, I didn't make that decision. I didn't run and I didn't hide. I didn't go into the bush and say every person for themself. It showed that leaders are people who are willing to put your life on the table. And I don't mean just myself. Throughout the sectors, women in those fields took care of marginalized populations that were most at risk in long-term care and homeless shelters and hospitals. Those are female-dominated fields. Women throughout the world were standing out and saying, "I know I might die, but I'm willing to put my life on the line to make sure that I save other people." I couldn't be more proud of all of them. Women do think that way. We've always been caregivers. We've always put ourselves second in taking care of others....

It's also been hard with the findings of all the children. Indigenous people knew those children were there from the beginning. We've often talked about their stories. I think there will be a bigger focus now. I'm a strong advocate that we can't hide our history anymore. It's in the history books of the NWT, but it's not in the schoolbooks everywhere yet. Indigenous people will take their place. I've talked to Trudeau and the other premiers already. Now we need to focus on trauma, mental health, and addictions because they are a result of the residential schools. They are a result of colonization. Now that it's out there, now is the time. I am expecting big changes. I'm expecting that governments right across the country will focus on the social and mental health needs of the people.

KATE GRAHAM: What has the response to that message been like?

CAROLINE COCHRANE: The premiers around the table have learned to be very careful with me. I'm Caucasian-looking, you know. People always argue with me and say, "No, you look Indigenous," but I see my father's skin colour. I don't see my mother's skin colour in me. It's my own perception. But when I first became premier, I don't think they knew I was Indigenous. I did hear a few comments that were very inappropriate. I actually had to stand up and clarify a few points. I won't go too much in depth because it's politically not correct. But I think the premiers learned that not only am I a woman leader, I'm a strong woman leader. When I hear things that are inappropriate at that table, I will challenge them. I don't care if I'm the only person challenging—in fact, I have been the only one a number of times. Premiers across the country have learned to be careful with their words. I think it's good. "Fake it till you make it" is another saying from one of my friends. If they have to fake it that they are not racist, that they are not sexist, that they believe women have strengths, that they believe people of diversity need to be in politics—well, I don't care if you fake it all the way through until you believe it because once you believe it, then you make it. Society has put us in little boxes. This is what women do. This is what people of diversity do. And it's time for all of us to challenge that because we all have strengths and we all have weaknesses and because of your colour, your gender, your sex, it does not make you less or more. It just makes you who you are.

KATE GRAHAM: What's next for you? What's on the agenda for the Northwest Territories?

CAROLINE COCHRANE: Now it's back to business. Covid, hopefully, is under control. We know that it'll be with us for life, but at least we're not seeing the numbers that we were a few months back. Now we're pulling out those priorities that we had when we were first elected and trying to get as much done within the last two years of my government. When I came here, housing was my priority. I was tired of low-income people not having homes. People ended up on the streets. I made a commitment to review every single policy on housing within our government and we have somebody who's in charge of that. I also worked with the minister to make a commitment that every Indigenous government will also be at that table. When we do a policy review, every Indigenous government will have a say. That's a start. That is reconciliation. The Truth and Reconciliation report says that all programs should have input from Indigenous governments. We're starting with housing. We're also big into self-government. In the Northwest Territories, more than 50 per cent of our population is Indigenous. I always say the key within self-government is self. So, if I make all the choices for the NWT, then I'm a hypocrite. I see the federal government, the Northwest Territories, and Indigenous governments all together as equals. If we can start that on housing programs, then it'll be hard to go back. I think that'll be the beginning.

KATE GRAHAM: That's a really important shift. What advice do you have for women who are thinking about stepping up to lead—in politics, or in other ways?

CAROLINE COCHRANE: You deserve to be here, no matter the skills you have and the challenges you've faced. Women represent 50 per cent of our population. If we don't have women at the table, we will never have a representative voice. You don't have to be perfect at everything you do. You don't need to know the answers. All you need to know is how to find out the answers and people are there to help you with that. No matter what you say to yourself, no matter how many times you doubt yourself, keep going forward. Challenge yourself. Even if it's not for you—and for me, it wasn't about me. It's for the generations of women to come. Do you want women to always be in the position that we're in now? That we celebrate that we had a majority of women in the legislative assembly for the first time in history, even though it's 2021?! What you decide to do with your life will affect the generations of women to come. Even if it's not politics, whatever role you take, remember that you are a role model for others and you are opening the door for generations to come.

NELLIE COURNOYEA

PREMIER OF NORTHWEST TERRITORIES
(1991-1995)

At the outset of the *No Second Chances* interviews, Nellie Cournoyea was the person I was most excited—and intimidated—to meet.

It took a bit of work to find someone with a direct connection to her. I tried the territorial government which was, understandably, hesitant about passing along personal information. I tried organizations she had been involved with, with similar results. Finally, I called someone who ran a small business in Tuktoyaktuk and said I was looking to connect with Nellie to invite her for an interview. Did the person happen to know former Premier Cournoyea?

"Nellie? Of course I know Nellie. Everyone knows Nellie. What's your number? Let me give her a call and I'll call you right back."

This began what unfolded as a rather unusual interview arrangement process. Nellie agreed, and I gave her a call. We had a lovely discussion and even over the phone I could tell that this interview would be enormously insightful. I proposed a date when we could travel to her and asked the usual details:

Location? "Along the ocean. Just ask someone. You'll find me."

Time? "Doesn't matter. It's always busy."

The production team at Canada 2020 was less than satisfied with these details. I was asking that we spend thousands of dollars on a series of flights for three people (myself, Aaron Reynolds on audio, and Adam Caplan on video) to reach the most northern place in North America accessible by road. We would fly as far as we could to Inuvik and then rent a vehicle (or hire a taxi, as we later learned, given the highly challenging road conditions in February!) to head north on the newly built two-lane highway. Our video and audio equipment filled several large hockey bags, an expensive venture on such small planes.

Booking accommodations also proved a challenge. End of the Road Inn seemed to be the only option in town, with fewer than ten rooms. I called to make arrangements and tried to secure our rooms with a credit card.

"Nah. We don't take credit cards in advance. I'd say it's fifty-fifty on if you actually make it up here, so if you do, we'll sort it out then."

With some pleading (particularly to those managing the project budget), we held our breath and booked our flights. The planes got progressively smaller and the check-in with large bags of equipment and many batteries got progressively more expensive as we went. We were grateful for the tip to book a taxi for the final leg of the trip over the highway, which as far as we could see at one point was mostly a guess on the location across the vast, white expanse, particularly once we were north of the tree line. Our driver asked us where we were going, and I was reminded that we didn't exactly know.

"Any chance you know Premier Cournoyea or where she lives? We're meeting with her."

"Nellie? Sure. She's my cousin."

As it turns out, Cournoyea lives in Tuktoyaktuk, an Inuvialuit hamlet in the northern Northwest Territories, in a home backing onto the Arctic Ocean—where even today, in her eighties, she casts her own fishing nets out back.

Cournoyea was born in Aklavik, Northwest Territories in 1940 and is a residential school survivor. Elected to the territorial legislative assembly in 1979, where she held a variety of cabinet positions, she got her start in politics through active engagement in highly contentious land claims negotiations. She once famously vowed to wear a dress if the Inuvialuit agreement was ever signed. She kept her word, arriving at the 1984 signing of the Inuvialuit Final Agreement in her friend's skirt.

In 1991, Cournoyea was selected by her colleagues (under the consensus government model) to become premier. She served until 1995, when she chose not to stand for re-election. She has received numerous honours and awards in her life: Order of Canada, Order of the Northwest Territories, honorary law degrees, and more.

We arrived at her home around 8 p.m. It had been dark for hours. Cournoyea opened the door and I apologized for our late arrival time (although we had spoken on the phone throughout the day, and she seemed unconcerned—and entirely unsurprised—by our travel delays). "It's good you're here now. If it had been earlier and the fish had been biting, I wouldn't have had time to talk to you."

We ended up staying for several hours and she was every bit as insightful and inspiring as I expected. By the end, she was showing off the arts and crafts of local women. She was helping to grow their businesses, using her home as a storage for their goods. All three of us purchased work before we left. It was an interview and an experience we would never forget with a woman who, in my humble opinion, is undercelebrated as a truly remarkable Canadian leader.

"It was an evolutionary need to do something about something." Nellie Cournoyea's first political work was fighting for her Indigenous community's control over land and natural resources. She was Northwest Territories' first woman premier.

NELLIE COURNOYEA: Living in the Arctic at my age was entirely different. The expectations that families and large family groups have of you are well established. I grew up on a trapline, coming into town every now and then, and on the off season, harvesting. Even as a young child, when you came to town you were expected to participate in all the gatherings that were going on. So, you're always hooked into the community. There weren't a bunch of kids just running around and not doing anything. In those days there was no government, so everyone fended for themselves; harvesting wildlife and getting the food source from the land. And that's the way I was brought up.

KATE GRAHAM: What was the earliest memory you have of being interested in some form of politics?

NELLIE COURNOYEA: I wouldn't say that I was ever interested in politics, as politics is known. Because you were expected to take part in your community and participate and you were taught to listen to what was going on. There were a lot of changes very quickly. Listening to the elders or the older people was a prerequisite. It was very important that you have to look after the elders and do what they say. You were always around people who were making things happen. It may not be political or great in some people's eyes, but it was survival. Having to live in a survival society, you get taught a lot. You're aware of a lot and you get very conscious of what's going on around you, and because of the environment we lived in, the participation of everyone was very important.

KATE GRAHAM: Let's talk a bit about the early days of your career. You worked in the media, and you were also involved in negotiating land claims and so on. Can you tell us about some of your early professional experiences that perhaps prepared you for one day becoming the premier?

NELLIE COURNOYEA: Well, it's difficult. We have lived in such a different environment. Your motivation for doing things are almost programmed for you. You know, it was not something you sought out. It was an evolutionary need to do something about something. And so, it was not a plan, or it wasn't a desire to be a politician or to be in the system, as you call it. It was never like that at all. It was a need to do something. I was involved from a very young age just being around people; elders and people who were doing things. That really made it real. It was not artificial. You learned how to live with people and respect people. And a lot of times we were away from each other....

When we came into Aklavik after a hunting season, there was a lot of work that had to be done because people all of a sudden came together. It was so exciting. People came from various traplines. It was very exciting to see all the people who you didn't see for a year, sometimes two, and so to be there and asking and wanting to do something with them was really a natural part of your heritage, you know? My mom was a product of the residential school. She was a laughing person, a happy person. She was also a product of the whaling industry. She met my dad, and they became man and wife. I was second eldest, and my brother was oldest. But we never really settled in one place until I was about five years old. We just wandered around. I mean, you have to be at the places where you're harvesting....

I suppose it's a different kind of awareness. I don't know how you'd translate it in today's life. And things were changing a lot. We come to town and there was a small radio station that people who were living in Aklavik put together. So right away it was, you know—you're on the air tonight and you're on tomorrow. We didn't put any great flag on it. You'd sit there and turn a switch. This way's on and that way's off. Then somebody came in to sing or to send a message or entertain someone out on the land. That was the radio.

I started on that. I know one time I was really in a rush. I didn't want to be there, and I sat there for an hour, did what I had to do, played some music and found out I wasn't even on the air. Somebody complained, "What's wrong? You don't know how to run this radio station?"

KATE GRAHAM: [laughs] Well, I guess it's good to know people were listening.

NELLIE COURNOYEA: It was very simple. [laughs] In community activities, particularly in Aklavik, you are really expected to be involved all the time. People coming together, and we didn't have any running water or anything like that. Everything was haul. The wood was cut. The water was hauled. All the food was secured from the land. Pre-preparation of food. It was always very busy. It was a time when everyone in the family was needed. You wouldn't have to say, "What are we going to do with this kid today? What are we going to make them do?" It was not that at all, you know, it was a continuous involvement with any part of the family. And being the second eldest and the oldest girl in the family, I was my mom's second hand—cleaning diapers, you know. There was a lot of work to be done. It was a different kind of environment. When you ask me some of these questions, it's difficult because it's so different. It's normal for me. But I mean…to try to explain it to someone else…. I was there, we had to live. We had to survive and that's what we did.

KATE GRAHAM: It sounds like this drive for survival also became a part of your personal values. Can you walk me through what transformed that kind of motivation into your first step into formal politics—when you became a member of the territorial assembly?

NELLIE COURNOYEA: The oil and gas industry had come up in a big bang, a really big bang. We really weren't expecting it. The government had decided to move Aklavik and create a new town called Inuvik because they said Aklavik was sinking. But it wasn't entirely for the people. They wanted to have an airport. A large airport. They selected three sites, for example. Where Aklavik is, it's right up against the mountains and they couldn't get the runway. That created a lot of disruption to the community. And so, there was a lot of, I would say, politics going on. You know, weighing how are you going to manage the change? How are you going to make that change over? And there was a lot of struggle because all of a sudden people who had everything in their control looking after themselves, the outcome of their own efforts, all of a sudden there was this pressure to—and an enticement, you know—to go into a wage economy....

It pulled a lot of people in. We didn't call it a political issue at the time. It was more a very grave concern, you know? What is going to happen? There was a lot of disorientation. There were a lot of bad things happening—too much liquor, not much involvement of local people. Although they tried very hard to set a standard. "Look, we'll help you out. Just don't do things the way you're doing." And then, "You're making a lot of dependence of people on government without their effort. So, you're creating a dependence." There were a lot who were concerned about that. I suppose I got involved as a young person with some older women because I was willing to be there and run around, and I found it really great. I learned a lot from them. And so, I think that without any real plan, with the moving of the community, and the oil and gas industry coming in and all of a sudden discussion about ownership, land, who should do things what way, who was in charge, how were decisions made, was really, really, absolutely taken away from the people who were totally self-sustaining....

Then, almost at the same time, there was a big movement for anti-trapping, anti-harvesting wildlife, too. It was a big struggle, and it took a big toll. There were three people in Ottawa who were really just giving the permits out. That's all there was to it. And where they went and how they went was not something that we had any control over. So what do we do? How do we—how do we gain some control back? That was probably the biggest push.

We had a lot of meetings with other Aboriginal people in southern Canada. They didn't have the claim settled but they were also involved with trying to get their base back on track. We went all across the country trying to learn what was going on, and found the best way is to try to grab hold of our control over the land because that was the most important. That's where everything came from—our life cycle was always around harvesting. It did not have anything to do with greed or anything like that. I guess that's where we decided we were going to institute an organization to negotiate land claims. I was working for CBC in Inuvik for a number of years before that. We set up our organization, a Committee of Original

People's Entitlement (COPE), and we had very strong people on there. We had to do it ourselves and we had to do it without being tied to any constraints. We had the support of the Alaska Native people who are going through with their final throes of land claims, and an Indian group down in Seattle asked if they could help. They loaned us a little money. But we didn't work for anything. No one was being paid very much so it was not a big slice. We set up the claim and that's the only way we thought we could go....

It was gruelling because we were the first off the mark. We had a lot of people who were concerned we were getting there first. A lot of union people felt that we would set precedents they wouldn't like. Territorial government wasn't really a legislature at that time. We knew Nunavut was coming. We knew that. There's no way of running around that, so people were at a standstill. Well, let's just hold it. Don't let anything happen, you know. Be nice. Be quiet. You know, appreciate what you're getting. But the words were shallow. And so we went through with the claim. I think I would have been kicked out of CBC anyway because even the simple things we did were being considered radical. But it was not radical....

We had an overall claim with all the other Inuit in Nunavut because we were still one territory. But we were pressured against a wall. Each day, the federal government was releasing more land, and subsurface lands, to the oil and gas industry. We were really, really privileged because there were a lot of very well-educated people who came to our region. We made good friends with them, you know. And they were honest and said, "Well, the economics..." They would tell us things. They weren't our lawyers or anything, but they had seen this type of action before. So, we had a lot of free and good advice and learned to understand what the heck was going on. That's when I heard that word, being political. Say something not too nice and it's political. It's honest but it's political....

We were negotiating the claim and then Nunavut decided that they weren't ready for it. Which was true, because they were spread out. There wasn't really any pressure for them to settle. They had more time. But each day going by, we had more alienation in our region. The direction from government was, once a permit was issued on a certain part of the land, the companies could work. It was getting tighter and tighter and tighter. So, we separated from Nunavut and started the regional process for a land claim. It took us ten years to get there....

I worked in there as we were negotiating. The territorial government would throw in all kinds of concerns. "Well, what about this? Well, what if this happened forty years from now? What about this?" Most of them couldn't even think beyond this year. There were a lot of spanners put in the discussions. And so, it was determined that somebody had to go into the legislative assembly as an education. It was not a fight but an educational thing, so when something came up, then there would be an explanation for it. There were about four of us who could go and by that time I was the only one who was most free; the other three had families. "Well, Nellie, you better try it." So that's how I got to be in an elected position at the government of the Northwest Territories. It wasn't any grand plan or something I desired to be or anything like that. It was just to counter a lot of the misinformation.

Sometimes it was very purposeful because they didn't want to see a land claim settled. And they didn't think Native people would be able to handle it. Well, the only way you couldn't handle it was if they gave you a poor settlement. No one could handle it anyway. That's how I got into territorial politics. It was a four-year term and I thought, 'Well, maybe a year, maybe two.' But then things kept happening that butted against the territories. I'd been all across the Northwest Territories and Nunavut several times. I knew all the communities. If you help them, they help you. There always was that exchange. It's what is best for the people, it's not what's best for yourself....

Then finally, in 1984, the claim was settled. And by that time, it was really hard to keep on going. Then there was the implementation process that was almost equally hard. And I thought, 'Well, should I leave?' There were a lot of discussion about that. There were some good people that could have got in, but you could tell that their heart really wasn't in it. You've got to be pretty tough, you know, to go up against a lot of people who are much smarter than you, much more educated in the system. I began to have some of the cabinet portfolios. I was so extremely lucky because I had known a lot of people and great senior administrators and bureaucrats. I had a lot of help from them. I was very fortunate always having a team. I was privileged in that. I would never have been able to do the things I did without them. So maybe I was in the right place at the right time.

KATE GRAHAM: I am in awe of your humility. I know you say you were "the most available one at the time" or "right place, right time" but your very genuine drive to empower people and address the injustices happening—enough to make quite a personal sacrifice....

NELLIE COURNOYEA: It wasn't a sacrifice at all. You did what you had to do. You were taught that way. Later in life people would ask me, "What do I have to do to get in politics?" I said, "You have to have a burning gut to do something. You'll get torn down very quickly, psychologically and mentally. You really, really have to believe in something and what you're doing. You have to have a target." But like I said, with all these people we had gradually built that target.

KATE GRAHAM: You said you ran to provide an explanation or a different perspective—but did you personally find it tough to make the switch to where, all of a sudden, you were in a position of power in the territorial assembly? Did it change how other people perceived you?

NELLIE COURNOYEA: I don't think so because it was much different than your government. It's a consensus government and if you really believe in consensus government you have to really work at it. Your knowledge base has to grow as you move along. You're continually trying to catch up. We were dealing with some pretty sophisticated institutions with national interests. This is just a small little place, but all of a sudden there was an insurmountable expectation that all the oil and gas reserves were here. So, we had a lot of different and contradicting interests. I never really had a chance to think about it because it was such a continual effort to keep up and keep ahead of the flood. The way I looked at it, if there was anybody who could help me, I just grabbed them right away. If they knew more than I did, I said, "Come here and be my friend...."

I was brought up where what you were told was what you were told, that was real. What you had to find out later, the more advanced you got in the political field, was that a lot of people didn't really tell you the truth or shrouded the truth. What does he really mean anyway? What is he saying? He's saying this but doesn't act that way.

I was an ordinary MLA the first four years. I didn't want to be anything else. Then I got into cabinet positions. But I am very, very dedicated to home base. I never neglected communities. I was always with them. I didn't evolve to a higher status where I only mixed with the Gucci people of the world. I believe sincerely that if you want to succeed when you're determined to do something, you get the best team you can around you—and I don't mean only academically important people, but the real people. You've got to be with them because that's your foundation. It's always your foundation. So, my life never really changed that much. I came home quite often. I live at home, and we still do the same things as when I was a premier. People stayed with me. My home was always open and that's the way I wanted it because that's my strength....

So being a premier, now, there were a couple of people who wanted to be premier the same time as I did. It was pre the Nunavut split. I had a lot of history with Nunavut and people in the eastern Arctic. We trusted each other, so there was a lot of give and take. We ran, and I became premier.

KATE GRAHAM: Was there much focus on your gender at the time? That would've been the first time a woman became the premier of a territory, and only the second time in Canada that a woman became a premier.

NELLIE COURNOYEA: No, not really. I don't know. It was not really discussed because I'd been around a long time. Because lots of times I can do just as much as a guy. The only time that it ever came up was when CBC wanted to interview me. [laughs] I never thought about it, you know, I never thought that. I think most of the males were smarter than me in academic terms....

KATE GRAHAM: I highly doubt that.

NELLIE COURNOYEA: Yeah, but they helped me. Maybe that's because there weren't any women there. But those were the people who were the most involved and understood politics. They helped me a lot. I really believe that when I came home, there was never ever, "Oh you're the only female in there." Never had that discussion. I think maybe people just thought, "Well, so what? You should be there. You're a person."

KATE GRAHAM: Then why do you think we don't see more women? The territories have all had a female premier—which is more than we could say about almost half of Canada's provinces in 2019—but when you look at members of the assemblies in the territories, women are still a very small percentage, around 15 per cent right now. Why do you think that is?

NELLIE COURNOYEA: It's been a man's territory for so long and it's hard to change that. That's the reality of the situation. It never worried me, you know; the men think it's their world. It evolves, sure, it all evolves over time. But it's going to take some time and it's taking too long. I think women have to have more confidence. Not as a woman, but as a person. And have more belief in themself as a person, not as a woman. It's great to be a woman. That's not to say there's nothing wrong with that. But I believe there's too much talk about gender and that I think that intimidates women. It contributes to the intimidation of women not being there. Because I see a lot of women running for political positions and what gets them is they don't really believe enough that they can be there, and they get tangled up in the knots of male-female. I don't know, I guess it's hard for me to explain. But, when something exists for so long, for centuries, from the woman being clubbed over the head, pulled by her hair, told to go and make the fire or something like.... To today, how much different is that? Women really keep the families together. The men are important, but the women are the ones who keep the family together and that's the way it always is. And I don't understand it in another way.

KATE GRAHAM: Do you think that, too, will change?

NELLIE COURNOYEA: No. I don't think so unless men start to have babies.

KATE GRAHAM: What advice do you have for women who are thinking about getting into politics today?

NELLIE COURNOYEA: I always tell people, get your experience from the bottom up. A lot of people are really working hard with their academic achievement and I'm proud of them and that's great. But get it from the bottom. If you're just in politics, that's why people make so many bad decisions. They don't know who the people are. They don't know who they're working for. So, if you start at a community-based institution that's helping people, work like heck on that. Once you start doing something, you'll roll with it. It'll come to you. And you don't have to fight for it. You're not fighting because you want to get somewhere. But what your attitude has to be—you want the people that you represent to know you and you want to know them. It's going to be difficult in a large Toronto constituency, but even up here, we have a lot of people who get in politics, and they fail badly because they haven't worked from the grassroots up. And always think about what you want to do. What do you want to accomplish? Don't think about, "I want to be there." If you start thinking that then it's about you. It has nothing to do with you. It's got to do with your community and how your community is going to survive in the best way they can in a broader society and a bigger society....

You know, when we decided that we were not going to survive—and I am using much more sophisticated words than we would at that time—we decided we were not going to survive the assimilation process. We'll never survive assimilating. It'll always be turmoil and bad feelings and discord. So, what we did is, we formed our institution representing the land we know best, which is Canada. We're part of Canada. So, you establish that, and you look after that.

KATE GRAHAM: I have to ask. You were in Charlottetown for the Confederation. What was it like?

NELLIE COURNOYEA: Well, it was hard work. I guess I knew all the senior politicians then and I was never excluded. As a matter of fact, when there were some issues—is this the right way to go in the Arctic?—I was included in those discussions. There were a number of other people who were involved with Indigenous people. I was in territory. I never saw myself separate from the two, you know, it's all in one. I worked with some pretty influential people, and no, I never was excluded, I was never behind the door.

KATE GRAHAM: You've been referred to as one of the mothers of Confederation.

NELLIE COURNOYEA: [laughs] I wouldn't want to give birth to a lot of those people. If they were my kids, I'd have some reckoning to do.

KATE GRAHAM: [laughs] I think if I said that to a man about being the father of Confederation, I don't think that would have been the answer.

NELLIE COURNOYEA: Well, life changes a lot, you know? And it's important to find a meaning, a real meaning. And when you understand that meaning, that will give you so much strength and ability to reach the objective. But I always tell people, "Don't get in there because of yourself. You're only a vessel in that particular position to help people. And so, never, ever really deny yourself or think that you can't do it. You can. But it's going to take time. It's going to take effort and you've got to start at the bottom." And that's, to me, so important for people. Cause nowadays, I think people are really hungry to believe that somebody really cares rather than just playing a politician.

PAT DUNCAN

PREMIER OF YUKON
(2000-2002)

You can learn a lot about someone by visiting them in a brand-new office. The walls may be bare and the bookcases still empty, but a few objects of utmost importance have made their way into the space.

I interviewed Pat Duncan not long after she was appointed to the Senate of Canada. We met in her new Ottawa office, surrounded by boxes in varied stages of unpacking. I couldn't help but notice that among the most prized objects that had already found their way to the top of her desk was a ragged piece of fabric.

"You know that expression 'Been there, done that, washed the car with the T-shirt?'" Duncan asked me. "Well, for me, this is the T-shirt."

The front reads, "No woman, idiot, lunatic, or criminal shall vote." It's a quote from the 1890 *Election Act of Canada*.

Duncan was given the T-shirt as a gift from a friend long before the future premier started her career in politics. Unplanned, her husband happened to be wearing the T-shirt on the day in 1996 when Duncan first filed her nomination papers to run for the Yukon legislative assembly. The fabric is well-worn and frayed. The Duncans have literally used it to wash their car, and now it sits in an office of the Canadian Senate.

Duncan was born in 1960 in Edmonton, Alberta, as the youngest of five children. Her family moved to Whitehorse, Yukon, when she was four years old. She married, became a successful business

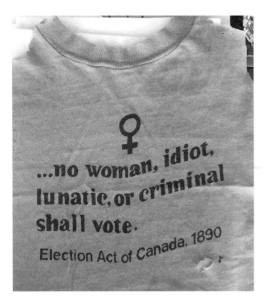

...no woman, idiot, lunatic, or criminal shall vote.

Election Act of Canada, 1890

The T-shirt.

owner, worked in media, and served as executive director of the Whitehorse Chamber of Commerce. Her path into politics includes a few notable twists. First, Duncan found out she was pregnant with her second child just shortly after filing her nomination papers to run for a campaign that ended up almost perfectly overlapping with her pregnancy. The election was called three days after the birth of her son. Secondly, Duncan entered the Yukon legislative assembly in 1996 as one of three Yukon Liberals elected. The other two caucus members were father and daughter. Duncan became the leader and ultimately led the party to victory in 2000, becoming the first (and to date, only) female premier of Yukon. The morning after the election, the *Globe and Mail* ran a story about the Yukon election announcing the new premier as "Mr. Pat Duncan," assuming the leader was a man.

Two years later, Duncan called an election. The party lost all their seats but hers and her premiership ended. Duncan was defeated as party leader in 2005, but this, however, turned out not to be the end of her public service contributions. She was appointed to the Senate by Prime Minister Justin Trudeau in December 2018.

Pat Duncan has an air of kindness and humility that is surely part of her political success. She has a clear knack for making people around her feel welcome and at ease, even when sitting amid stacks of unpacked boxes. She knows who she is and what matters to her; she clutched the tattered T-shirt panel as she shared her story.

The *Globe and Mail* called her "Mr. Duncan."
She was told to change her lipstick. Pat Duncan
faced overt sexism as premier of Yukon.

PAT DUNCAN: Well, I think my interest in politics stems from my family of origin. I'm the youngest of five children and my oldest brother is thirteen years older than I am. By the time I came along, I was almost an only child because my siblings were so much older. My mother used to say, "We made all the mistakes with the other ones." And, you know, the youngest child tends to get away with a little more. So, I had a different relationship with my parents, and I had the example of these bright, older brothers and sisters. We used to have great dinner-table conversations. My father—I'd call him a feminist even though married life was very different at that time, with a different role for women at home, and I can't recall Dad doing a lot of cooking or cleaning or anything like that. But he was a feminist in the sense that he really believed in the strength and intelligence of women. As I said in his eulogy, he would say, "They can because they think they can, Patricia Jane." That was his attitude with me. "You think you can do it? Do it."

I was always that kid on student council. Communications and journalism were more my bent than politics. I grew up listening to the news, talking at the dinner table, having conversations with people, and being active in school. My curling team went to the Canada Winter Games. The other three on the team were quite shy, so it was, "Well, Pat, you go and speak on behalf of all of us." That's the role that I've always either gained for myself or been given, and it's just a role that fit me.

KATE GRAHAM: You had a successful career leading the Chamber of Commerce and being active in your community in all kinds of ways. What led you to take the leap to run for office?

PAT DUNCAN: When I was working at the Chamber it had been suggested that I run for mayor. I had a very wise friend who said, "Pat, stop and think. Is it you or is it your ego that's running right now?" So I didn't run. Then I was asked by the Yukon Party, and I said no. I really felt strongly that there wasn't room for women's voices at the table. It was very much a male-dominated party, and I didn't feel included. And then it was suggested that Ken Taylor, who was the leader of the Liberal Party at that time, approach me. I got involved with the party and with the party organization. I had attended a [Progressive Conservative] leadership convention—actually, the leadership convention where Brian Mulroney won—and I liked politics. I like the organization of it. I enjoyed my time. Ken phoned me and said, "Could we go for lunch?" I said, "Well, you're trying to save money for an election." So, I made him lunch. He tells that story on occasion. He just asked me to consider getting involved and I felt heard. I felt that his vision of a Yukon was one I could share and contribute to. I also believed that the cabinet table needed women who knew what it was like to have to buy a box of formula, or a bag of diapers—what it was like for women. When he asked me to run, I thought about it. My husband and I talked about it, and we were contemplating having a second child at that time. I said, "What happens if I get pregnant?" He said, "We'll figure it out." And lo and behold that's how events unfolded.

KATE GRAHAM: [laughs] Okay, so you've got a very young child and you're thinking about having another, and you're asked to run, and you say yes. You then find out that you're pregnant with your second child. At any point in there did you consider that maybe, maybe this wasn't the right time to do this?

PAT DUNCAN: I did not. I didn't, and I'll tell you why. I have many times since—as only women who are moms, who are so good at guilt, can do. For a long, long, long time I thought, 'Oh man, should I have done that?' Then I go back to the family of origin. Being the youngest of five, my mom had gone back to work after we moved to the Yukon. I would have been four or five. My husband's mother, who was ten years younger than my own, had gone back to work within days of him being born. And so that was how we had grown up—with working moms. That's what moms did. Fast forward—and it's within my lifetime and the lifetimes of my nieces and nephews that we've gone from maternity leave being a number of weeks to up to eighteen months. Now it's a totally different time. It's going to sound trite, but it just seemed right at the time.

As it turned out, we were able to make it work because my mother-in-law stopped working. Our daughter developed a very close relationship with my mother, and then our son was born, and he was very close to my mother-in-law because she was available at the time. And she got to stay home with this baby in a way that she didn't get to with her son. I have had that conversation several times with my children, [asking them,] "Do you think you suffered?" And I get this "What are you talking about?!" Because it was just what Mom did. That's just who Mom is. When I used to have my moments of angst about it in the premier's office, I had this staffer who would say, "You're teaching your daughter and your son what women can do and what women are capable of. This is an example you're setting for them." Okay, I'll take that. It was of some comfort to me at the time and it still is.

KATE GRAHAM: In that first campaign, with a young child and another one on the way, how did motherhood factor into your campaign experience?

PAT DUNCAN: I was going door to door ahead of the election being called and I was wearing a parka. The key was going door to door so that people had seen me. When the election was called, I'd just had the baby. I remember one particular door in my riding. Bearing in mind that I'm postpartum and this is, like, day twenty-something of a thirty-day campaign and I'm just tired. One of the Yukon Party campaigners had been going door to door in front of me, saying, "Well, you know, she just had that baby." It was a common refrain. I went to this door and a woman said to me, "Didn't you just have a baby?" I stepped back and I just—lost it is probably too strong a word—but I stepped back, and I said, "You know what? If this was a man coming to your door, you wouldn't ask that question. Tony Penikett's wife had twins when he was running." She stepped back and said, "Oh my, I am so sorry. I have been a lifelong feminist. I'm sorry I asked you that question." I believe she voted for me.

KATE GRAHAM: I hope she did. So, you won your seat, but your leader, Ken Taylor, did not.

PAT DUNCAN: There were only three Liberals elected: Jack Cable, his daughter Sue Edelman, and myself. Trying to lead a party from outside the legislature, it's very difficult. The party had high hopes going into that election. Jack had been there for a long time, so he became our interim leader. The frequency with which Jack would happen to run into the leader or some of the members of the Yukon Party in the washroom and then come back and say, "This is what we'll do in question period...." It surprised me a little. Then there were the references to "the Hen Party over there" from Minister Keenan, who subsequently apologized in the legislature. Later, when I was premier, they made the comments, "Oh, the premier's just gone shopping in Calgary." Not 'she's promoting a pipeline;' 'she's shopping for a new wardrobe.' Those sorts of comments. I had a person who worked on my election campaign tell a story to my children recently. She would get phone calls, "Will you please tell Pat Duncan to change her lipstick?" And she'd say, "Did you hear what came out of her mouth?"

"No, she just needs to change that lipstick."

I can recall the snarky comments from the Tories during the election: "We can't let those housewives be in charge." I also recall one media conference in the cabinet room. I came in wearing my kilt and one of the reporters said, "Oh, you're wearing your kilt today." And his colleague, a female reporter, said, "The premier doesn't comment on your ties. Why are you commenting on what she's wearing?" Self-policing is what is needed, not the speaker saying you're out of order. I'd like to think we've come a long way. I'm not sure we have.

KATE GRAHAM: That's a big question. Tell me about your path to become the leader of the party. It's quite an unusual set of circumstances.

PAT DUNCAN: It was close to the end of the election. Ken approached me and indicated that he wasn't confident that he would win his riding, and he hoped I would step forward. And as it turned out there were three of us elected. As much as I respected Sue and Jack, I wasn't wanting to work under a family dynamic like that with either one of them as leader, so I put my name forward.

It was short-term thinking at that time. I wasn't thinking, 'Oh I'm going to become the leader and the premier.' It was just, 'Here's the immediate task that has to be done. We need a leader and we've got to get through this session, and we've got to build the party. We've got to continue to build the momentum and build towards the next election....'

It was so busy. So busy. Recruiting candidates. Every step you take in the legislature, every motion, is building to the next election and building the party and appealing to Yukoners. It's like putting building blocks in place, but you have to build on a solid foundation of your principles and your party's principles.

KATE GRAHAM: You were the first woman to lead a party in the legislature and then go into a general election. Do you remember it being important at the time that you were a woman—either as a pro or as a con?

PAT DUNCAN: I don't recall that being an issue or a pro or con during the election—but the *Globe and Mail* referred to me as Mr. Duncan. That was funny. A reporter from CBC and I were walking in front of a well-known bookstore on Main Street. And we went in to get the paper and just laughed about it. But I had too many other things to do. It wasn't that I was elected leader of the party and the party was already in power. I had actually won an election. That part was exciting, but truthfully, I was so focused on, 'Okay, what do we do now?'

I remember going to my first premiers' conference. I was like, "Oh my goodness, how am I going to do this?" I received the very sage advice that, you know, every one of those people got there the same way you did—one vote at a time. I found them easy to work with and accepting. They were all willing to listen to what I had to say, and it was a good working experience. I think I stood out a little bit in the Team Canada missions. I can recall going through the Vancouver airport at one point in time and this woman was trying to stop me and just asked in one of those casual conversations, "What do you do for work?" And I just said, "I work for the government." And she said, "You're that woman premier!"

"As a matter of fact, yes, I am." [laughs]

KATE GRAHAM: "That woman premier."

PAT DUNCAN: Yeah. "That woman premier." I mean, when you look at it, women's roles have changed a great deal. Men have not had as different roles. Politics, it's not for everybody. It's really not. This life is not, well—nothing worth doing is easy. It's not easy and it's not everybody's cup of tea. My husband would sooner walk across hot coals than ever stand in front of people and talk, but I like to share ideas. And if it's something that I'm passionate about, like the Yukon, I will stand up in front of anybody and talk. There was a particular set of circumstances that worked in my favour, and I was able to do this thanks to an amazing number of people.

KATE GRAHAM: What would you say to a young woman who is thinking about running, maybe who has a young family or is already feeling busy and under pressure but wants to be able to contribute more. What advice would you give to her?

PAT DUNCAN: I had a unique situation. I would ask, "Have you got support? Have you got the foundation there to help you? It's a hard road with a young family." The world has changed so significantly even in the time since I've left politics in the Yukon. I mean, social media wasn't around when I was in office. I'm not sure I would recommend it for someone with a very young family in today's circumstances.

KATE GRAHAM: If you could go back, would you do it all again?

PAT DUNCAN: I would. I would because I've had this conversation with my children. I asked my son if he thought perhaps the example of his grandmother and myself and my mother-in-law, if that perhaps has coloured his perception of women. He has a sense of women as very self-sufficient and independent. I had a staffer who came in and sometimes brought her daughter with her, which meant that I had toys in my office. She'd spend time there. Later, this woman went to work for the next premier. Her young daughter came in and said, "That person can't be the premier because he's a guy!" She told me that story some years later. So, then I knew I had made a difference.

KATHY DUNDERDALE

PREMIER OF NEWFOUNDLAND AND LABRADOR
(2010-2014)

In 2013, Canada had six female premiers. Former Premier of Newfoundland and Labrador Kathy Dunderdale laughs when she thinks back to this time.

"I remember being at an event with everyone and Alison Redford, or maybe it was Christy Clark, got up to speak, and said, 'You know, we've got them surrounded.' And we did! We had women leaders from coast to coast."

This moment would not last long. By the end of 2014, several provinces had replaced their first female leaders with men once again—including Alberta, Québec, and Newfoundland and Labrador. By the end of 2015, there were three female premiers left at the table. By 2019, there were none.

Kathy Dunderdale was born in Burin, Newfoundland and Labrador, as one of eleven children. She first became engaged in politics in the 1980s as a citizen, successfully lobbying Fishery Products International to reverse a decision to close the Burin fish plant. After that, Dunderdale was elected to Burin Town Council in 1985 and later served as deputy mayor. In 1993, she left town council to run in the provincial election against a sitting cabinet minister. She lost. When she ran again in 2003, she won and was invited into Cabinet. In 2010, Premier Danny Williams retired and Dunderdale was sworn in as interim leader of the Progressive Conservative Party. She was eventually elected as leader and led the party through to victory in 2010. In 2014, she resigned as premier and retired from politics altogether. To date, she remains the only woman who has served as premier of Newfoundland and Labrador.

A visit with Dunderdale is every bit of the Atlantic Canada experience one would expect: welcoming and hospitable, full of stories about people and places that offer a taste of life in Newfoundland. From the local jam and freshly made muffins, to the home filled with photos of her children and late husband, to the impressive range of Newfoundland and Labrador books on the coffee table, meeting with Dunderdale in her home environment offers great insight about the woman and the leader she is.

"When decisions are being made that affect
your life, you need to be at the table to speak."
When Kathy Dunderdale was premier of
Newfoundland and Labrador, she was one
of six women at the premiers' table.

KATHY DUNDERDALE: I come from a big, rambunctious family. I have ten siblings and a mother and father who were incredible parents. Our house was a great place to grow up. There was lots of love, lots of laughter. We saw them have great challenges in trying to raise and educate us all. We knew how important they were to each other. And we knew how important we were to them. We had parents who were interested in their community and in the world. What went on in our little town was important. When people needed help, people responded. While sometimes it was a struggle to feed us all, there was always room at the table for one more. We never had so little that we couldn't share some of what we had. And that was true not only for our family but for the community. We realized very early on that we needed one another, that we depended on one another, and what happened to one was important to all of us. We had a responsibility—although it was never phrased that way—to try to be part of a solution for people who had less than we did. That's political action, whether we knew what to call it or not....

My mother always had an interest in what went on in the larger community. She hadn't lived her whole life in Burin. She had lived and worked in the city in service for years before she was married, around powerful people who had enormous control over the lives of the people in this place. And she was a very intelligent, articulate woman and she had views. She'd like nothing better than engaging in a discussion about what was going on in the world. It was quite normal for us to hear debate about what was happening politically in the province and so on. And we were always encouraged to join in if we had something to say.

KATE GRAHAM: Tell me about the fish plant.

KATHY DUNDERDALE: Our community, like so many in this province, was dependent on the fishery for our economy. We had a deep-sea plant in our town since 1942. This was in the 1980s. That plant had fuelled the expansion for the company, so they were able to build plants in other communities and expand their enterprise and do very well, certainly substantially better than a lot of the people who worked for them. The way the system was set up in those days, it was called the co-adventurer system. If you had fish, everybody shared in the profit. But if you didn't have fish, if you came home from a trip without fish, many of the men who had worked hard for weeks without success came home without a paycheque. That caused a great deal of difficulty for a lot of families for many, many years. I know my own father tried to get away from the fishery so that we could have a more stable income and he could look after his family in a consistent and sustainable way. He was never quite successful. He fluctuated back and forth through his whole lifetime....

The fishery, like most commodities, have their highs and lows. In the 1980s, we were going through a particularly rough time. It was determined that there were too many people in the fishery, too many fish plants, and so on. Governments and companies were working together to consolidate the industry, which meant that people had to be let go and that plants had to be, too. We had to work for better economics so that the fishery could survive and sustain a significant part of the population. But they decided to close the plant in our community. We felt strongly that we had been the backbone of their survival and their expansion. We argued that, while we didn't have shares in the company, we certainly had a great deal of sweat equity. And that had to be taken into account when people were making decisions about what our place was going to be in this new organization and this new industry. We began a citizens' action committee and barricaded the plant and the ships and their product. [laughs] We said, "You've got to talk to us, and we have to negotiate, and we have to come to a reasonable solution. Otherwise, what is here remains here in the hands of the people." We involved everybody in our communities. We came together, we organized, we lobbied, we made our arguments, we did our research. We supported one another. We were always prepared to listen to what people had to say and offer solutions where we could work together. After a sustained effort for over a year, we were successful in keeping the plant open. It looked different than it did before. It was no longer a primary fish processing plant. It was a secondary plant doing secondary processing. But it carried on for another thirty years providing income to people in our communities.

KATE GRAHAM: And you emerged as a leader through the process. It's been cited as your departure point into politics. What was it about that experience that made you decide to take the step to run for office—in your case, to the local council?

KATHY DUNDERDALE: It reinforced for me the need to be engaged; the need to be aware of what is happening around you. Governance affects every part of your life. It affects your children, their education, your healthcare, your infrastructure in your community. Everything. And it was clear to me that those processes had to be informed. When we talked about saving our plant, we had to tell the people who were making those decisions that they have an impact on us as people. All of that needed to be taken into account, and they couldn't have known any of that unless the people who were involved spoke to them and told them their story. I think for me that was the most powerful lesson at that point, that when decisions are being made that affect your life, you need to be at the table to speak to it. Because life impacts us all differently and unless there's that awareness, I don't know how you can make decisions that are meaningful, effective, representative, and productive. Otherwise, you're imposing something as opposed to building something.

KATE GRAHAM: Tell me about your first or your early days in politics. You're a newly elected town councillor. Did you experience sexism? What was the experience like?

KATHY DUNDERDALE: I experienced sexism every day. It was all around me. I was a young feminist. I had seven sisters and three brothers. People often asked me, what was the makeup of my family? I would say, in our family, there were eight girls and three kings.

KATE GRAHAM: [laughs]

KATHY DUNDERDALE: My wonderful brothers didn't appreciate that very much. But there was a big difference in the way our parents treated us. And to me it was amazing, isn't it? Because my mother was the only girl in a family of six. I think she often thought that she was liberated—even though she wouldn't have expressed it that way—because her girls were able to do the things she was never allowed to do. I railed against the fact that I couldn't be on a soccer team, that I couldn't be a leader in the school. I would ask, "Why not?" and it was, "Because you're a girl." Early on I started to rail against that. I didn't accept it and I wanted the same opportunities that my brothers had....

I married a sailor. My husband was a master mariner and so he spent a significant part of his life at sea when we were younger. We decided to build a house. When he was away, I went to the construction site to give direction. I had two small children and was heavily pregnant with my third. My father went to speak to the construction guy first. As I walked over, my father said, "My daughter will be here shortly." The guy kept responding and saying, "Yes, that's okay. But where's the man? Where's the man that's building the house?" And my father keeps saying, "My daughter is coming and she's building the house and she'll be here." And he kept saying, "But where's the man?" And I said, "I'm here now." And I'm coming as big I can be with a kid on each hip. I remember him turning and looking and saying, "Oh, a goddamn woman."

And, you know, I've never forgotten this. If I was not homeless at the time and with my parents, I probably would have fired him on the spot. But that was the world I lived in back in the 1970s. It was everywhere. So certainly, I found it on the council. I adopted early on that you have to accept people where they are. Sexist attitudes come from old ways of thinking and acting. And until you challenge people to look at it differently or give them a persuasive argument as to why they should examine their approaches and thinking…[you] can't do any better if you don't know any better, as Maya Angelou famously said. So, for me it was important to accept people where they were and begin to show them how things can be done differently. To challenge them in a respectful way. I found that a lot of the anti-women rhetoric was fuelled by fear. And if women somehow got something, that meant you were losing something. It took time, and it takes time for people to realize that when one of us does better, we all do better. You can't shut out half the human race because of their gender or because of their skin colour or because of anything else. It's foolishness. A rising tide lifts all boats. And when that realization takes hold, I think it all becomes a bit easier.

KATE GRAHAM: You became deputy mayor and then the first female president of the Newfoundland and Labrador federation of municipalities. What led you to take the leap and jump into provincial politics?

KATHY DUNDERDALE: My first foray into provincial politics was 1993. As president of the federation of municipalities, we were having a serious disagreement with the provincial government about how municipalities were funded. They brought in a new formula for allocating funds, and they did so without any consultation with municipalities. I wasn't very happy about that. I felt that somebody had to take a stand. We had a popular government at the time, and they were in many ways for the people of the province. But there were still serious issues about being heard. The [Progressive] Conservatives put a great deal of effort in convincing me to run, but they had a Tory MHA [member of the house of assembly] in the district in which I live. I couldn't run against one of our own. But in the next-door district they didn't have a candidate. We did a poll and I think I had eleven points. [laughs]

KATE GRAHAM: Oh, perfect. [laughs]

KATHY DUNDERDALE: It was just one of those things. Why was it open? It was open because none of the men wanted it. We didn't have a chance. But they kept saying what they really needed was for a high-profile name like me to give them some momentum. Whether or not I was successful was another matter altogether. I knew I was going in without a chance of success. But with lots of convincing I decided to do it. Perhaps my own vanity drove that more than good sense. And once I went and got the nomination by acclamation, my support seemed to drift away from me. I was left on my own in a district I didn't live in, in which there was no organization and there wasn't any money available to me. So, amid the tears, [laughs] I had to decide whether I was going to continue this, or would I try to cobble together some kind of a campaign and see what I could do. And with the support of a few friends, we set out. It was hard because you're trying to maintain your dignity in all of this, too. I would get in the mirror and have a chat to myself before I would call the campaign headquarters to talk to the provincial campaign manager. My instructions to myself was, 'Don't you cry, don't you cry on that phone.'

KATE GRAHAM: Did you always listen to that advice?

KATHY DUNDERDALE: Yes, I always managed to get through the call. Because if you got off the phone and cried, it would kill you. So, you could do what you want now, and you can do what you want after. But you have to be professional on that phone. So, anyway, we put together our personal funds to find a place to stay and get a campaign office. We found new friends and supporters in the community.

A dear friend of mine made a huge sacrifice to come and be my campaign manager; he was so important to me in those early days launching my political career. Men have been important in my life, all my life, in doing that. I have great men in my life. I have always had great men in my life and never would have gotten to the places that I was able to without them and their support. And my friend Luke was one of those. Well, once he took the burden off me about the organizational pieces and process pieces, I was able to get out into the community and go door to door and talk to people. I was hooked. It was the most wonderful experience. People are kind and generous and they're great liars, too, you know. But I think it comes from the best place because they don't want to hurt your feelings. They'll say, "Don't you mind all those Liberal posters on my fence." [laughs] I mean I just loved it. And people talked about the realities of their lives, and what it is they're looking for. And what people want is fairly simple: Living with dignity, having the means to a decent life, to have a good roof over your head and food on the table, the ability to educate your children, and access to healthcare. I mean, what most people ask for is not outrageous. They just need somebody to hear them and work with them. I just loved them. I wasn't successful although I made a good showing. I didn't embarrass myself. My mother said I passed. I stayed on the periphery of political involvement, like elected politics, for a number of years, but thought perhaps that my time had come and gone in terms of standing for election....

And then in 2001, I got a call from an organizer with the Danny Williams team asking me to be part of his leadership bid. I got involved again. And during that process, I was encouraged to consider standing for elected office again. I was able to contribute to the writing of the mandate and the platform, and I was enthusiastic about the people who were coalescing around the Williams team and what the focus was. I had a real belief that here was an opportunity to do something and to do it differently and to have a great effect, and that was very exciting. I had a fight on my hands for the nomination, but I was successful, and then moved on to election in 2003 in a district that people thought we would never take. The former MHA was seen as a man of the people and very popular here. But I did win the seat....

Coming to government really is a baptism of fire when you come from the street. All of us look at government from the outside. Not many of us are familiar with all the processes and responsibilities once you have the job: Learning how the house of assembly worked, understanding what my role and responsibilities were, coming into the department. You know, what did we do, how did we do it, what were the programs, and how effective were they? At first, all of it was shocking because I had worked my whole life in the community up to that point. Around social justice issues and so on. Now, I find myself minister of the lead business department. That's quite a shock to the system. So, you have to dive in and learn exactly what you're supposed to be doing. You get your mandate letter and then you have to do a full analysis of the programs that you were responsible for. How effective are they? What's the feedback from stakeholders using your programming, and so on? We came into government in a time when we were buried in debt. The bulk of our budget was eaten up by education and health. I remember all of those first six months being extremely difficult, trying to get your head around what you were supposed to do. And you're responsible from the day you walk in. You can't say, "Hang on now, give me three or four months for me to learn the job here." You have to be responsible on the [first] day.

It was long days and long nights. We needed a budget for March or April. It was an absolutely brutal process because the financial situation and the problems become very clear. We were broke.

And so now you're having to sit at the table and make decisions about whether people can have teeth, you know, whether we've got schools that are leaky, windows falling out. We've got air-quality issues. We've got people who need dialysis who are having to leave their homes and their families and everything they have to move to the city for treatment. I mean, the list just goes on and on and on. And you don't have the money to do any of it. These are basic needs, basic rights. I remember leaving the cabinet room and feeling a hand on my shoulder and turning and the premier saying, "This is not what you put your hand up for, is it?" And I said, "I'm so overwhelmed, I don't know what to do." He replied, "We can only take it off a piece [at a] time and do what we can about it and move on. And move on piece by piece by piece, we'll try to make it better and we'll find a way to do things differently. But that is all we can do."

That led us to doing the whole SWOT [Strength, Weakness, Opportunity, and Threat] analysis within government, and I chaired the economic policy committee at the time. We had to understand very clearly where our challenges were, where opportunities were, and what we need to build a sustainable future for this province and develop an action plan around that. It was an enormous piece of work and very satisfying. And you can actually build a road map about how to progress and look beyond four years. Because you can't do all that in four years. We have a significant role to play in it, but others will need to take this off as we go along. Everything else started to fall in place because that's what I cared about. I was passionate about the work.

KATE GRAHAM: Tell me about the path to becoming premier.

KATHY DUNDERDALE: Where to begin? I wasn't expecting the premier to resign. I had come to politics with him. I knew that his intention was to serve two terms. I thought I would probably go with him; when he had served his eight years and was ready to move on, I would probably be ready to move on as well. My husband had been diagnosed with cancer about a year before I ran for office, and he passed away when I was about two years in. That changed a lot of things for me and part of surviving that tremendous loss in my life was work. It was a way I could escape the grief that had surrounded me for so long. I was back to work within three weeks of Peter passing and the premier asked me to take on a new portfolio; natural resources. The one portfolio I thought I would never have and, you know, I remember not answering the question but saying, "Oh, somebody else should do that." And I was clearly told that the premier didn't want anybody else. I think because of my particular circumstances at the time, I wasn't sure if I knew enough. But I had just gone through one of the worst things that could have ever happened to me, and I was still standing. Nothing was ever gonna be worse than that, not even failure. And what would Peter say if he were able to give me advice? And he'd be pushing me in that door to do it. And so I said, "I'll try."

It was a very challenging and exciting portfolio. And because it was so busy and so demanding and so on, it gave me respite from my own sorrows for at least part of the day. It was an important time for me in lots of ways. I had to chart a new course for myself because of all the plans I had been making for years with Peter had now shifted in a way I never expected, and now I was on my own. I had to forge a new path. So, when the premier decided it was time for him to go, midterm, I knew I would stay until the end of the term. It was the first time I considered whether I might run again for a second term. I took over as premier and I wasn't intimidated by that at that point.

KATE GRAHAM: Really?

KATHY DUNDERDALE: No, because I had been deputy premier, and I had worked closely with Premier Williams and represented him at the Council of the Federation meetings. I had met all the other premiers. That first meeting was terrifying. I come from a province on the eastern edge of North America, with only a half million of us spread out over a vast landmass. My own experience of the world was somewhat limited. I was gonna sit at a table with just one other woman—Eva Aariak from Nunavut. I was grateful that Eva was there. That was comforting. The group was experienced. Well-established men. Politicians who knew a lot about issues in this country and were able to speak to them in a very articulate way and in a very confident way. It's daunting. And it was interesting. Within a couple of hours, I had a fairly good understanding of the dynamics at the table. I was comfortable. I felt, 'Okay I can do this.' So, I had that bit of experience under my belt when I went to the premier's office....

I remember when Premier Williams made the announcement in the lobby of the Confederation Building that I would be the acting premier. I can hear one voice clearly saying—and young—"It's our first woman premier." I've never really aspired to those titles and so on, but I remember a general sense of excitement. And I remember young girls being excited by it and reaching out to me. At the time, I was into running and I'd go early morning for a run before I went to work. We're a small place, so everybody knows everything. The school bus would pass me as I jogged down the street and the little ones in the window waved and shouted because they knew. It was wonderful. They wanted to come to the Confederation Building, and I loved it. Every time I had a moment and there were young people in the building, I would search them out and bring them up to the premier's office and I loved that they sat in the premier's chair. It was just so important for them. I would say, "You're sitting here today, perhaps you'll sit here again when you're older. Maybe you'll be a premier here." I knew how important it was for them to see a woman in this position doing this work and for them to understand very clearly in their young lives that this was something they could do. Because every man that I ever talked to, I'd say, "Have you ever consider running for political office?" And I can tell you that I can't remember ever speaking to a man who ever said, "No, I haven't." I would approach women and they would say, "Who, me?" without exception. They never saw that it was a choice that was available to them or something to be seriously considered. That it would just automatically be in your array of choices in your life, particularly with little girls to say that this is perfectly normal for you to be here in this office.

KATE GRAHAM: It's so very important. Tell me about the leadership race.

KATHY DUNDERDALE: There was lots of noise and then lots of pressure on me to reconsider my decision not to run for the leadership. The plan was that I would do the interim premier role and then I would go back into Cabinet. I thought to myself, 'Perhaps the speaker's chair might be something I might aspire to.' That's how I was thinking. I will oversee this process while my party gets itself reorganized now around leadership for the next election in 2011. I was ignoring the calls for me to reconsider not running. I had my own list of things that I really didn't want to do. I didn't want to do a provincial tour. I didn't want to do a televised debate. I didn't want to carry this responsibility all the time. There was a group within my own caucus who had concerns even about my interim role. I started to get messages that I needed to be careful about what I was doing. That my concerns with women's issues were well established, and some were expressing concern about that and whether or not that would predominate the decisions I would make. It just made me angry. It was extremely annoying. I'm busy and I really don't want to be dealing with this foolishness. And it just really got to a point that I got completely fed up. And I thought, 'I just need to push back. If this is what's going on here, then there's more work to be done than even I realized. I'm not happy about this and you're not going to be happy if you really believe the things you're saying to me because I'm gonna change my mind. I'm gonna run.' And that is honestly how it happened.

KATE GRAHAM: Wow. So, you run for leader....

KATHY DUNDERDALE: I immediately told the people closest to me. Within a couple of hours, we had polled a majority of the caucus, and I had their support. I think some of the other stuff had probably come from a small few who had ambitions of their own who thought I might change my mind about running and were trying to create an argument that I wasn't, because I wouldn't be well received. But the whole thing completely backfired on them. I had more than enough support to go forward. I was surprised at how excited people were about it all. I didn't wait for the appropriate time to make the announcement. I decided to do it a different way. I just went to a scrum and said, "This is what I'm going to do," without having all the hoopla and so on. And so, we began. Leaderships in and of themselves are very divisive, very difficult. They can have lasting negative impacts as you go forward. The whole process is troublesome. But, for the most part, we got through it all pretty well.

KATE GRAHAM: And then not too long later, it's time for the general election. You were running as the sitting premier but hadn't been out for general election yet as premier. Did your being a woman feature as part of the election narrative?

KATHY DUNDERDALE: I don't remember it. In terms of my own party, I mean, I was it. If we were going to win, we had to win with me. And I had also developed a talent of ignoring annoyances because that's what that would have been to me at that point in time. I wasn't gonna be baited into a discussion about whether or not a woman should be premier in the province or whatever. I would speak my truth as to the value of full participation of everybody in our province in the political process.

KATE GRAHAM: Let's roll the clock forward a little bit. You win the general election. Everybody's excited. And then at some point things start to fall apart—and this is a central part of this project because it tends to happen much, much faster for women. Tell me your perception of what happened.

KATHY DUNDERDALE: We've seen it in a variety of ways in our own country and internationally as well. I think it's much of the same phenomena we saw happen in the United States with Barack Obama. They thought outside the box and did something differently. They elected a Black man as president in the States. I think they're very similar in terms of the expectation that gets built up around what you expect from them and it sets us up for failure. I don't think people have the same tolerance. People make mistakes. We all make mistakes. You're not asking to be elected because you're infallible. You have ideas about how you can effectively change things to make life better for all of us, whether economically, socially, or whatever. Once you get there you'll find challenges that never crossed your mind, or fiscal situations that you didn't understand to the same degree just because all of the information was not available to you. And so, you have to adjust and so on. But if things aren't going exactly the way that people think they ought to be going, then the fault is yours—that you have miscalculated in some way. People have less patience with women or with whoever the new person is around that stuff because they took a chance and gave you the opportunity, and you haven't met their expectations. So they're not prepared to stay with you as long. And perhaps it's just because people are paying more attention. I don't know....

In politics, we tend to be all A-type personalities. We all have strong ideas. You wouldn't run if you didn't have strong ideas about how the world ought to be. Most of us think we can make pretty good premiers. And so there tends to be, well, there can be a great collegiality if things are going well amongst a group of elected officials in a party, for example. There is also a great deal of competition. Because most people don't want to sit on the backbench. They want to be at the cabinet table. When things are good, things are usually pretty good. When things start to go sideways—and the polls are usually the first indicators of that—then things can get rough. And things can get rough in caucuses. And it doesn't take much. In our first term, we were in a full-fledged strike of public servants with 40,000 people out on the street because we were offering zero, zero, zero, zero. Basically, we were bankrupt. It wasn't well received, and people were outraged. It was rough. People would be in the galleries, and they'd be shouting down at you. and they'd be saying awful things about your mother and your relatives, your children and your pets. You lost your innocence pretty quickly about what you were dealing with here, and then people become worried about their own political futures. The sands shift—or, you know, as they say here—the water on the beach starts to change. And when people start to think more about their own survival, a political party is not the venue where people are going to set all of that aside for the greater good. That's not how politics works, and I don't care what party you're in. It's what's politically expedient....

People are asking for daycare and extended daycare and better programming for their children and better educational facilities and recreational facilities. And all of those requests are legitimate.

Perfectly legitimate. But you're not able to meet them all and you just don't have the means to do it. But in making those decisions you tick people off, depending on where that is in their list of priorities. It's like having a toothache and your friend having a toothache—you're not particularly concerned about how much pain he's in so long as you've got your own pain to deal with. That's the nature of it. So, governments can grow old quickly and people can get frustrated, and you've always got somebody on the other side saying, "Hey, look at me. I can fix this. I have the better idea...."

It was so difficult for the people who love me. I talked to my children and my husband about what I wanted to do, and I was supported wholeheartedly in my choices. I talked to some degree to my extended family, and they encouraged and supported me. But the effect that this has on them pains me to this day. I'm tough and I knew that I could take it. You shouldn't do this if you don't have a good sense of self. You really are stepping into an arena. There are no two ways about it. And I have enormous respect for people who step into that arena; it's the people who are up in the stands that you need to be worried about. I was in office when social media found its place in the world. I remember the premier turning to me and saying, "You heard about this thing called Facebook?" That was 2004. Then everything exploded. I'm sure none of the views expressed were new, but for the first time in our lives we all had to hear about them. We were inundated with every thought that ever crossed anybody's mind. So, when anybody levelled criticism at me, I was more than prepared to stake out my own piece of ground and defend myself, but for the people who love you, to have to listen to people who work every day at tearing your arms and legs off, saying the most hateful, spiteful things—it is very, very difficult. They don't have any kind of a way to respond. And they hurt for you in a way that you don't hurt for yourself at all. It's just part of the situation in which you find yourself. But it is so difficult. I know that members of my family carry deep wounds from that and, you know, it never really goes away because you never get your anonymity back. I want to encourage people because we need good people now more than at any other time. But I also have to say, "Prepare yourself because it can be wicked. It can be really tough. It can be really tough on your family."

KATE GRAHAM: I'm not from Newfoundland, but I have often heard people talk about the whole "fighting Newfoundlander" as sort of a defining political idea out here. Do you think the climate of politics is particularly tough — or particularly tough as a woman?

KATHY DUNDERDALE: No question about it. In Newfoundland, we're consumed with politics. Many, many friends, colleagues, and co-workers have remarked to me, when they've moved from the political arena here or working for government to other parts of the country, how quiet it is.

KATE GRAHAM: Really?! [laughs]

KATHY DUNDERDALE: Here we talk about it on talk shows just about all day long, five days a week. There are gatherings and coffee shops from one end of the province to the other where people gather every morning to have a talk about current events and what's going on. Everybody has a view. While there are some great insights that will come from all of that, generally it tends to be a case of the blind leading the blind. But everybody has an answer. Everybody knows how it ought to be done. And it would be wonderful if some of them threw their hats into the ring. I think it was Roosevelt who said he welcomed people into the arena who were prepared to take on the fight to do what needed to be done, but he wasn't particularly interested if you were up in the stands either sharing enthusiasm or criticism. You need to be engaged. And I have a very similar view, I have to say. I encourage people to have thoughts and to state what they are, but it can't just be taking people apart by their arms and legs who are out there in the arena trying to do something about it....

I'm more interested in people who say, "I want to be a builder of community." I want to encourage people to find opportunities to become engaged in that process. I want them to be inspired by the issues and the need for change rather than a political ambition to sit at a table. There's a wonderful book I encourage everybody to read. It's called *Random Passage* by Allan Porter, and it speaks to the early days of Newfoundland and the role that women in particular played in the development of this country, eventually, and now province.

Men worked hard and they worked hard at very particular jobs, the fishery, and it was all-consuming. It fell to women to organize community, to organize families, to be assistants to their partners and their husbands in the building of an economy. There was no part that their life didn't touch, and they were amazing, incredible women. I read that book at least once a year because it tells me who I am. What my heritage is. What I'm made of. I'm so proud of the strength and the resilience and the love of family and community that are captured in the pages of that book. I don't know how we got to a place where women had doubts about our ability. We all grew up with incredible women in our families, in our communities, and there are wonderful stories about all of that. And how we got to a place where the seed was set that perhaps there wasn't a role for them in everything we do in this country puzzles me. We don't have to dig very deep. We don't have to go back generations and generations and look at the role that women played in the development of Newfoundland and Labrador. It's such an aspiration and an inspiration. When I was premier, I often talked about the fact that my grandmothers would be astounded that their granddaughter became premier. That was such a leap. I mean for them, catching a glimpse of somebody who might come on a boat as part of a political campaign or to catch glimpse of a minister or a premier would have been a lifetime experience they talked about forever. To ever imagine that anybody that belonged to them will be a part of the government, it was beyond any concept that they might have had. Their granddaughter became the premier and maybe that's because of all the work they did, underneath, in the history of Newfoundland and Labrador....

You need to own your place. You have to understand that you have a right to be at the table and to be heard. That's only going to happen if you make it happen. You don't lead, you know, you can't assume that others will take care of your interests if you're not involved and if you're not engaged. And so, if you're interested in your own well-being and the well-being of your family and being part of a community, you have to take responsibility for that and for all of us. You can decide where your place is going to be. Not everybody has to stand for elected politics. But maybe you need to support somebody who's going to. Maybe you need to inform somebody who's going to be at that table. There are other things you can do. And you can raise your voice in any number of ways. But if we're going to have politicians who are answerable to the people they represent, you have to be engaged. Otherwise, you just put up with whatever happens. And that never works well. In Newfoundland, we say a rising tide lifts all boats. When women do better, when we embrace diversity, then we all do better.

PAULINE MAROIS

PREMIÈRE MINISTRE DU QUÉBEC
(2012-2014)

My introduction to Pauline Marois came in 2012. On September 4, 2012, the Parti Québécois won a minority government in Québec, making leader Pauline Marois the first female première ministre for the province. As Marois delivered her victory speech at the Métropolis in downtown Montréal, a man entered the building with a semi-automatic rifle and tried to assassinate her. The gunman killed a stage technician and injured another individual before he was apprehended by the Montréal police. I can remember seeing the video on the news of Marois later returning to the stage and trying to calm the crowd.

Marois is something of a legend in Québec politics. Born in a working-class neighbourhood in Québec City, she was raised with her four younger siblings in a house built by her father. Marois excelled in school, yielding her a scholarship to attend an elite, private Catholic girls' school. In her memoirs, she describes the experience as a "culture shock" to be surrounded by girls who came from a life of privilege and affluence—and that the experience had a major impact on her professional choices and personal outlook from that point on. She attended Université Laval to study social work, then completed a Master's of Business Administration at HEC Montréal, and began working in social services, leading the childhood services division at the Centre des services sociaux du Montréal métropolitain. Her entrance into politics came in 1981, when she was elected as one of only eight women in the National Assembly of Québec—and gave birth to her second child just eight days later. What followed was a career of remarkable endurance with more than thirty years of political service. She ran unsuccessfully to lead the Parti Québecois in 1985 and 2005, and then became leader in 2007 when she ran unopposed. She served as leader of the Official Opposition from 2008 to 2012 and then led her party to victory with a minority government in 2012.

I contacted Marois at the outset of the *No Second Chances* project, foolishly (and in retrospect, rather arrogantly) sending her an invitation letter in English and signed by an English political scientist (me). This was not lost on Marois. We received no response and later found out that she had little interest in participating in an English podcast with an Anglophone host. Frankly, I should have known better. We asked if we could arrange an interview with her and a Francophone journalist and said we would run the interview largely unedited and entirely in French. She agreed.

Noémi Mercier, a Radio-Canada journalist, agreed to conduct the interview and host a special *No Second Chances* episode to ensure that listeners could benefit from hearing Marois' remarkable story. The audio interview is available as a podcast episode on NoSecondChances.ca. Marois' story is remarkable in many ways, as a rare example of someone who has bravely faced some of the most difficult things a person can go through in politics—from assassination attempts to political defeat—and yet found the strength to keep on going.

"If you do not listen to voiceless people, then
one day you'll pay for this poverty very dearly."
Former social worker Pauline Marois went into
politics to help the marginalized in Québec.
As a member of the legislature and as premier,
she led the way in balancing work and family life.

INTERVIEW

NOÉMI MERCIER: Good morning, Madame Marois, and thank you for accepting this invitation.

PAULINE MAROIS: Good morning, Noémi. I'm happy to talk with you.

NOÉMI MERCIER: We always wonder what it takes to encourage women to have more political ambition. Essentially, how do you become a female premier? Let's go back to the sources. Your family background—you do not come from a particularly well-to-do environment.

PAULINE MAROIS: I come from a very modest family. My father was a mechanic. My mother was teaching elementary school at the time. She had a preparatory studies degree A or B. After your ninth year, one can teach in a one-room school. One thing however, she really valued education. I think it's in this kind of school that I developed a taste for engagement. But I was coming from a modest family. Nobody had been in politics in my family. Neither my father nor my mother could have imagined that I would one day become a member of the national assembly. Becoming premier was not a possibility in their mind.

NOÉMI MERCIER: Did you ever imagine that you would do that, not just be an observer of politics or be subjected to it, but be a participant in the process?

PAULINE MAROIS: It was at the end of my adolescence, at the beginning of my adult life, that I decided to participate in the political process. I didn't know that it would lead me where it did, and of course, at age twenty, I hadn't decided to be premier of Québec. But I began to work with social assistance beneficiaries.

NOÉMI MERCIER: You studied social work?

PAULINE MAROIS: Yes, I studied social work at Université Laval in community organization and I wanted to save the world. But seriously, I wished for people to have a better life. So, I found myself in the Outaouais, a region bordering on Ottawa, where obviously, the French language was under attack; in the seventies, when they wanted to assimilate the Francophones of this region—in particular in the Outaouais, where it was prevalent on a daily basis—and, sometimes, I had difficulty understanding some expressions people were using. So, I went to work there with social assistance beneficiaries, and I ended up concluding that we absolutely had to change the rules of the game to allow these people to play a meaningful role in society and become recognized citizens and not marginalized citizens. This is where it came from. But there were also a few other things—the October Crisis was very important in my life. The proposed changes to the comprehensive social policies of the major social institutions. Claude Castonguay [and] Mr. [Gerard] Nepveu of the famous Castonguay Commission, wanted to propose major changes to the financial aid program to the people, which ended up being the comprehensive healthcare insurance plan. And I wanted to defend the social assistance beneficiaries because they, in my opinion, didn't have the resources that they needed to live well or properly. I used to participate in demonstrations carrying signs against Mr. Castonguay when he came to the Outaouais, and I went to a public meeting, during which I asked questions. I remember very well the kind of questions, like, "If you do not listen to voiceless people, one day you'll pay for this poverty very dearly."

NOÉMI MERCIER: And you were what? Twenty? Twenty-one?

PAULINE MAROIS: I was twenty-one and finishing my course in social work at Université Laval. I was an intern in the Outaouais because my husband worked there and, as it is said, "qui prend mari, prend pays" [she who takes a husband takes his country]. I participated in demonstrations there. I ended up concluding that if, one day, I really wanted to change things, it's in politics that the power and decision-making reside. I was twenty-one, that was my way of thinking, but in the absence of not only female role models in my life, but also models of political involvement, I pursued my life by doing social work in community organizing, in social development, and by trying to lend power to voiceless people.

NOÉMI MERCIER: Why did the issue of voiceless people, the poor, marginalized people—why did it touch you so much?

PAULINE MAROIS: Why did this touch me? Because I was under the impression that a society was wasting its talents, its intelligence, its imagination.

NOÉMI MERCIER: And you had examples of this close to you?

PAULINE MAROIS: Yes, I had examples close to me; friends, people close to my family. I also thought that there were formidable potentials that would not flourish. It didn't mean becoming a well-known researcher or premier, but at least being able to hone one's talents, become a good skilled worker, a good artisan. My father was in this predicament because he was a very smart man and very interested by everything happening in the public forum. It probably played a role for me, but there wasn't.... He was not politicized in a refined meaning of the word—he was a man interested in everything happening on Earth, and he read all the time when he came home after work. He was a very hardworking man, he was always reading his newspaper when he came to my place—he was a bit older—he read any magazine, he was always doing something, and he always regretted not having gone to school. It was his life's regret. His life's regret. At one point, he worked as a messenger in an office. Later, he worked as a mechanic. He had a few health problems. He found another job and he had to do accounting, on his own, and he was always afraid of making mistakes, getting it wrong. As a matter of fact, he couldn't remember if he had done a third or a fifth school year. And this was his greatest regret. However, it gave him the determination, he and my mother, to send us to school for as long as possible and to make us go all the way commensurate with our capabilities. It was the precious heritage that my parents left us. There was no difference between boys and girls; it was quite fascinating. Imagine, we were in the seventies, I was already twenty-one, and the boys did the dishes, their beds—oh yes ma'am—and even household duties, especially since my mother was ill for a while. My father and mother played a more traditional role. But for us, the children, we were all equals. Father would sometimes call me to give him a hand while he was repairing a truck or a car at home. He would yell, "Come and give me a hand. You must be able to do this." So, no difference between boys and girls; this surely left its mark on me. It did in my subconscious—it was quite forward-thinking. It was also not shameful to take care of a newborn, change diapers, and all those kinds of tasks. So, at home, boys and girls were raised to respect equality—although different, still equals.

NOÉMI MERCIER: This is great. If we jump a few years to 1981, your first foray in politics, you worked in Jacques Parizeau's office and then Lise Payette's. What convinced you to take this step at the time and run in the 1981 elections?

PAULINE MAROIS: In 1981, Madame Payette left; I was her chief of staff. As minister for the status of women, she oversaw two departments, and she was also minister of social development. Of course, I helped her recruit female candidates. She told me that she was leaving a year before she left. It was kept quiet within her office and by Monsieur Lévesque [the premier]. She spent all that time trying to find women who would run as candidates because, at that time, there weren't many women. Listen, I really don't know if there were more, in 1980, than six or seven women at the national assembly. So, I also worked on finding women, etc. And I concluded that, because I had followed my contacts from 1970, one day I would maybe be in politics, I told myself that I would, I would get involved in a riding where people would adopt me and support me because I was a Parti Québécois militant. I had been chief of staff—I had to have been a militant in the Parti Québécois, which I had been in the past—and I told myself that I would get involved and then run for a seat. And, by happenstance, Madame Payette left. There weren't many women candidates. Monsieur Lévesque, himself, called me, asking, "Why wouldn't you go for it?"

You should know that one of my good friends in the trenches thought that I had what it takes to do that and that I shouldn't wait. He thought that I could do it then, that I knew the Parti Québécois well enough, I had already been a militant and a chief of staff, etc. Altogether, this convinced me that, essentially, this is what I wanted to do and at the time, the thinking was that the Parti Québécois would be defeated. In any case, in my opinion, with everything I knew, I almost said no. But my partner, because we took all our decisions together, told me, "Listen. Why don't you do it? You want to change things; you want to be able to serve the women and men of Québec. Don't wait—you're being offered the opportunity." It took some pressure from the people around me. Amongst them were three men, but also a little bit [from] Madame Payette. Still, three men. And I was also pregnant, eight months pregnant. So, I dove in thinking that I would be in the opposition, that I would have time to get acquainted with my job. And if I saw that I was uncomfortable doing it, or that I was not qualified for the job, all I had to do was not run in the next election.

NOÉMI MERCIER: It didn't happen as you describe it. Not really. You were elected, the Parti Québécois was elected, and I think people forget the fact that your first experiences in politics were happening while your pregnancy was quite advanced. So, you were pregnant with your second child; you gave birth eleven days after the election. And you already had your daughter, who was two. You gave birth to a third child two years later, in 1983. You were still a minister. Two weeks later, you were offered a more important ministry, after your third child, and in 1985 you gave birth to a fourth child. In the following week, you ran for the leadership of the Parti Québécois. If this was happening nowadays, it would make the headlines.

PAULINE MAROIS: I think so, I think so. And people think that family responsibilities constitute a barrier to women's political involvement.

NOÉMI MERCIER: Why hasn't this stopped you? What were you thinking?

PAULINE MAROIS: Why hasn't this stopped me? I go back to the extraordinary collaboration between me and my partner. I often give speeches to women who invite me for a talk, and I often tell them that equality starts with cooking, feeding, and changing babies. Why? Because women feel spontaneously responsible for the family and the children. It is more difficult for women to cut the umbilical cord and convince themselves that their partners can also share the responsibility for the children as much as they do. And so, yes, I could afford to choose a profession, to become a politician, to participate. I was lucky, or I worked on getting this extraordinary chance of having a man in my life who shared all the chores.

NOÉMI MERCIER: He was easy to convince.

PAULINE MAROIS: Not necessarily. I helped him a little bit. I helped him because when we got married—we've been married for almost fifty years—when we got married, I didn't want to have children right away. And I told Claude, we'll have children when we're ready to have them and when we feel responsible, both of us equally, for the children that we bring into this world. And, for me, it was a prerequisite. So, for seven or eight years...I had children after nine years of being married. We shared the chores; there is nothing dishonourable in vacuuming, cleaning the counters, and washing the dishes as well as tending to the children's needs. And I have to say that, for me, it was a very important factor. I wouldn't have had the life I had on the political scene had I not had this partner. I say it again, the ten or so times that I have had the opportunity to say it, I tell women, "Don't feel guilty, but make sure that your partner is as involved as you are concerning the children, the children of the two of you." And that's what does it—at a certain point we can leave in the morning reassured because we know that somebody is available in case of a problem or anything and we, the politicians, we are bound by crazy schedules, etc. So, you have to choose your partner well if you want to participate in political life.

NOÉMI MERCIER: Yes, but society is also responsible.

PAULINE MAROIS: I worked very hard on this aspect too; society has a responsibility to encourage balancing work and family. I am very proud of the famous centres de la petite enfance [CPE, childcare centres] because they allowed this to happen for couples and especially for women, to allow women to get rid of the guilty feelings. I personally think that women should tell themselves, I have children, my partner and I have made children together, and he is as capable as I am of taking care of the children. By contrast, there is still some weight on our shoulders because we have to let go. Letting go becomes another obligation.

NOÉMI MERCIER: That's it. You were elected for the first time when there had already been four women ministers in the national assembly's history. You get there, you have two very young children, and you will have two more in the following four years. How did you manage to gain acceptance by your colleagues, not only as a new minister but also as a young woman and a young mother? How did the people around you react?

PAULINE MAROIS: I think that, at the beginning, people found it a bit unusual. They weren't sure that it was a good deal because some people, although they never said it clearly, did think it…. What is she doing here? Shouldn't she be taking care of her children? It was obvious. Yes, yes, it was obvious from their facial expressions as well as their demeanour. I thought that the way to counter this message they were sending me, the comments that I felt they wanted to make—they were also reluctant to see a woman hold such an important portfolio, to be responsible for a department, etc., especially when I was named to the ministry of labour and security of the revenue—was to work twice as hard.

NOÉMI MERCIER: Oh yes?

PAULINE MAROIS: Yes, yes. Honestly, I wasn't different from the others because—a lot of women will tell you this—when I had a meeting of the cabinet, I was very well prepared. I had read all my files, I knew all the data, I could explain everything. I had prepared my defence.

NOÉMI MERCIER: They couldn't stump you.

PAULINE MAROIS: They couldn't stump me, especially in cabinet meetings. I was the only woman at the time. Then, later, Denise Leblanc came. But for about a year, I was the only woman.

NOÉMI MERCIER: The only woman?

PAULINE MAROIS: Yes, yes, yes, and I felt that they were wondering, "What does she know about these matters?" Don't forget that I had returned to school. I obtained my BA in social studies, and I had also finished a Master's of Business Administration. This too is a part of the culture of women, to be self-confident, to seek new knowledge, to be more skilled, not to be stumped, and, especially, to regain our self-confidence. This was a marked lacuna in my life, even if I said that I was a go-getter, that I had done this and that, there was always a little bit of doubt, 'Would I be able to do this?' etc. So, I had two degrees. I went to cabinet meetings, I discussed my files, but I was still under the impression that my colleagues doubted my capabilities. "She can't know this better than us." Here is a funny example: While I was the minister of labour and security of the revenue, I had to make decisions concerning the responsibilities of certain trades. The steelworkers and the electricians had to work on the same project with well-defined functions, but the rules and laws were not clear about this. When the union representatives came to my office, they looked at me somewhat condescendingly, thinking, 'What does she know about our business?' So, I looked at them— I remember quite well Monsieur Laberge, who was in front of me—I said, "Monsieur Laberge, you can go to the other side, in the other building. My colleague is a lawyer, but he doesn't know more than me about your business, these trades. You're going to take me to a job site and tell me about it and I'll see what it looks like. So, when I come back, I'll be better equipped to make my decision. Educate me first." It's a bit of that. But I worked twice as hard, I think, to always be perfect.

To never be wrong is exhausting. It is exhausting. I call that the complex of the best in the classroom. It is somewhat disappointing. We shouldn't adopt such an attitude. Do we have any other choice? Sometimes, no. I think that at the time, I had no other alternative because I wouldn't have been accepted by the gang, and I wouldn't have had any say on matters and my voice wouldn't have been heard. On the other hand, it worked. Monsieur Lévesque had named me to sit on the priorities committee and removed me. I won't get into the details. Two years later, he created a committee to deal with the major economic crisis of 1982–1983. He called me back because, as a matter of fact, he heard me and listened to what I was saying. And also, I think that if I hadn't worked so hard, he wouldn't have taken into account my opinion and wouldn't have called me back into his strategic committee. It was fruitful, but very hard, very difficult [and] demanding. It was very unfair, and I don't remember which of my colleagues said, "An average man can be successful, [but] an average woman, it's not the same."

We always have to be better. There are also all sorts of studies, you know them as well as I do, there are a lot of studies that were made by large companies on gender, the roles that females and males play, and women's applications for jobs in companies. If she is under the impression that she does not satisfy 95 per cent of the requirements, she does not apply. In contrast, a man answers 80 per cent and says, "I'll learn the rest." It was proven and known, so it's been like this for a long time. I think there is an innate instinct, maybe, but it's mainly cultural.

NOÉMI MERCIER: If I'm right, you ran thirteen campaigns in all, of which two were for the leadership of the party and three were campaigns as leader of the party. What's the difference between these campaigns and when you fought for the premiership? How does the "game" change the perception that Quebecers have of you? Does the way you present yourself change?

PAULINE MAROIS: I have to say that, at times, I behaved in a masculine way. I say it quite humbly and simply. For instance, especially when I was in the opposition, I raised my voice and banged the table because I was told that I was too nice and incapable of beating Jean Charest, who was then premier of Québec. Never "This woman is too nice, too polite, too this and too that," when I was not forced to behave as they expected. But it did change things a bit, honestly. There were other things that I also had to put aside, as Madame Payette had taught me. I often say that people looked at my earrings, my hairdo, my scarves, my dresses. I like colours, I like fashion. I'm a bit exuberant. Madame Payette had written to me, saying, "Listen to me, buy a black dress, a grey one, a brown one, and forget the earrings and the scarves. They'll forget all of that and they'll listen to what you have to tell them." But it's cruel because women are often looked at this way. And sometimes, I was so appalled when I did this. It was a reflex. I told myself, "We never make these kinds of remarks to a man who has tailor-made suits by great tailors, who is always perfectly dressed, or others who are, pardon the expression, a little 'sloppy,' neglected, crumpled, and all the rest. But for a woman the perception is very different." So, I became premier, and I had a style of leadership that was rather unifying, even though I have had a lot of conflicts with some of my colleagues at some point. In my life, I am very unifying, and I affirm it wholeheartedly.

NOÉMI MERCIER: How does being unifying manifest itself?

PAULINE MAROIS: By listening and making decisions, and by taking into account the viewpoints of the people around us. At the same time—and that was also the strength of my leadership—I think that women are capable of this even if the guys think that we are not, that we are unable to make decisions in tense situations, where there is not necessarily unanimity. I was looking for consensus. I listened a lot and was willing to not always be right, because I believe that women's egos are a little less acute than men's. Men have more misery doing that. They can't accept that they're wrong. Listen, I accept that at some point I made bad decisions; I didn't make the right choice. I discussed with my team, with my departmental team, with my ministers around the council table, with my deputies. And then, it was really a great story between my deputies and my ministers. When I was in government, there had been some sad events before I got there, but I think that's what made the difference. And I'll tell you, when I was premier, I had fun and took a certain pleasure in thinking that I was going to do things that would change the lives of my fellow citizens. Yes, power. Power—and I am not afraid of power as a means. Power in itself can lead to dictatorship; it can lead to the worst situations imaginable. But power is a means. It has its limitations, however, and that was also my ability, to create that balance between changing things and then taking into account the pace at which you can do it. I didn't have everything perfect; sure, there were things where maybe I went a little too fast, but I think that was what made the difference with my style of leadership. Is it a woman's leadership style? I don't know. There have not been so many models. How do I know if it's more feminine? But it is still something that often comes up in the discussion of women in power. I had difficulty recruiting women candidates because they were afraid of power. Power corrupts, absolute power corrupts; no one can protect themselves. We can give you markers, tags, and then, no. And as long as we do not renounce the fundamental values that move us, and we set ourselves a goal, even [if we have to] make a little detour to get there, I think that we should not be afraid of power, which is a powerful agent for changing things; many major social policies, economic policies in Québec have been adopted by politicians, by governments that have changed the lives of Quebecers for the better.

NOÉMI MERCIER: I have the impression that there are two frames, or two representations of Pauline Marois that have existed in the media or that you have shown yourself. I found in interview notes that you told me once, "I am able to be killer if necessary, in the sense of slayer." So, the iron lady who is not discouraged, who breaks down doors, who is a pioneer. And, at the same time, there is another version who doubts herself, who has trouble with self-confidence sometimes, who seems more or less [un]comfortable in the role of leader. Which is the real one? Or are they true at different times?

PAULINE MAROIS: They are true at different times. When one is a policymaker, it takes a solid determination to pass through crises, opposition, difficult times, to try to mobilize people. Then you have to be determined. Then, at some point, indeed, I could be a killer in the sense of saying, "If I fail to settle down this person or to question this proposal in my party, we are not going anywhere," and then I risk not being able to carry out the project in which I believe, be it in the field of electricity transmission, language, or culture, whatever. That's what it means to be a killer, yes. For me it is really to make sure that the project I am leading is not compromised.

To be a killer is to be able to say "I want, I will win," and to win. Sometimes you have to step on a few toes, okay? And you even have to put aside people who can be harmful or who can prevent you from achieving the goals you want to pursue. It's hard but if you don't have the instinct to survive, you don't implement what you want to achieve. And then, at the same time, I am this woman who, when the premier entrusted me with mandates, I always said to myself, "Will I be able to carry out the new mandates? Do I have what it takes?" And even as a premier, when I had important projects to implement, I thought to myself, 'There, Pauline, breathe through your nose and then look for the most enlightened points of view, to check if I'm going in the right direction. And then I'm going to trust myself. And then I'm going to do whatever it takes to get there.' It's not bad, otherwise; it's when the lack of confidence prevents you from acting and creates such a trauma that you can no longer move, or that you can no longer move forward, or that you can no longer make a decision.

NOÉMI MERCIER: So, it can be constructive?

PAULINE MAROIS: That's right, the doubt can be constructive because it forces us to question things, and then maybe to find better solutions than those originally proposed. And that, once again, is somewhat related to the ego. On the other hand, in women it is more common than in men. But women are very much blamed for doubting themselves.

NOÉMI MERCIER: It's true. Sometimes it's not just a handicap.

PAULINE MAROIS: Yes, exactly, it can be turned to our advantage. You just have to know. It's as I'm telling you, from the moment it has a blocking effect and prevents us from moving forward, it prevents us from proposing things, from making decisions. This is unhealthy, and it means that you have to do a little introspection and say "No, no, no." Don't let yourself be influenced by your lack of confidence. You have what it takes and sometimes, occasionally as they say, there were people around me who were telling me, "Come on, you're able to do this or that. You'll convince him because there are all sorts of situations." Convincing a colleague that we want him to go there when he did not want to, this is an important task when you are premier or when you have a responsibility in an organization, no matter which. In the private sector, it's the same thing, so I was getting help in that sense. My husband was very helpful. It sounds funny but he was very helpful on the matter of his trust in me when he told me, "Listen, look at all the others around you. They do not have half of your training and a quarter of your experience, and they don't doubt themselves." But a little doubt is not always bad; it can help us to be better.

NOÉMI MERCIER: The "boys' club"—that's an expression that often comes up when you try to explain why women advance so slowly in the places of power, in politics. What does the boys club look like? What form does it have? What is its objective?

PAULINE MAROIS: We are not always very good negotiators. You're going to laugh when I say that we're not always very good negotiators. Usually, when men want—for example—to prove a point or get something, they will go and look for allies and build a strategy in advance. The "boys' club" [is because] they know each other, they worked together for a long time, and us girls, we are all alone there. We are two or three and have established a sort of complicity that, in my opinion, affected some projects in the last few years. I can tell you this because we felt that there was not always solidarity but complicity to say, "Okay, we will rely on each other and go in this direction, supporting such a project." But the members of [the] boys' club have attended the same institutions, they were on the same golf courses, they go to the same gym, they belong to the same social clubs, etc. Our presence in the public square is very recent. Men volunteered in sports clubs and in chambers of commerce as well as social clubs. Women helped children in hospitals and shelters, in community groups; there was less talk in the public square, fewer ties were developed in sports organizations, economic organizations. Again, we talk about the traditional role of women: we took care of the children and our parents, cared for them, and therefore we were less in a situation where we created these relationships. I would say that in the last few years, I think it has changed a lot because women are now present in universities, in CÉGEPs, everywhere. They are still a little less present in social clubs, [in] chambers of commerce.... Even if we have not seen some women become presidents of chambers of commerce, we see more around the table. But still....

Recently, I listened to the results of a study on the presence of women on the boards of directors of small, medium, and large companies; we are still around 20 per cent. The boys' club is also created in the financial organizations, companies, etc. So, there is a habit of working together, there is a knowledge of each other's values, and one can feel somewhat isolated when we wish to belong to these networks. I have seen women voluntarily build networks, in the sense of meeting regularly with women who came from economic backgrounds, social backgrounds, academia, and community circles to try to network together, but it was a bit artificial. It's good to network, it's good to share our experiences, etc., but the next day, when you're all alone on the board of directors or in the management of your company, and of twenty directors there are three women, you are still alone.

NOÉMI MERCIER: Absolutely. On September 4, 2012, there were two events that will always mark the history of Québec. Québec elected its first woman premier, and there was an attack that some characterized as a terrorist political attack that cost Denis Blanchette his life and seriously wounded another, Dave Courage. These two events are always associated. When you think about that night, what feelings come to you?

PAULINE MAROIS: There are two that come to me: A pleasure—namely that I was trusted—a pleasure and pride especially that I was trusted as a woman to lead Québec, and that I had a responsibility to meet the expectations of Quebecers. I immediately had this feeling, and then after, a profound sadness to think that I had been the target of a killer who could have made real carnage. You know his gun jammed. That's the only reason. Otherwise, he entered a crowded room at the backstage of the Métropolis Theatre, where there was my family, my colleagues, because we all expected to go onstage. After the fact, I would say I had a huge sadness, but at the moment, I will tell you, my reaction was to protect the people who were there. At the event itself, I wanted to protect the people who were there because I knew there was a real problem; I did not know of what size, but I knew that they wanted to evacuate the room.

NOÉMI MERCIER: You knew that same night.

PAULINE MAROIS: I knew that there had been an attack on people—that a person was killed, that a person was wounded, a few hours later. But at the scene, I saw that there was a major problem, especially since I was told that we had to evacuate the room. I saw fire. In fact, I saw smoke coming out of the backstage area, and I thought that if we evacuate the people in a haphazard way there would be a disaster, there would be victims because there were many, many people in the room; there was enthusiasm, but all the people would have been crushed.

It's not complicated. My first reaction was to say, you have to calm things down, and that's what I did to the best of my ability, I believe. As far as the attack itself is concerned, I don't know what to tell you, except that a lot of people who were maybe in other situations than mine, at the political and informational levels, would surely have used this event to promote themselves. I've always refused to do that. We proved this fact later. In the end, the judge said that it really was a political attack, and I never wanted to use this attack for my own purposes. I can tell you that there are people who blamed me, people who were close to me and who believed in our political formation, in our orientations. What other political leader would have suffered such an attack without using it for the purposes of "I am a martyr?" I never wanted to do that. First, out of respect for the Anglophone community because he was an Anglophone who shouted, "The English are waking up!" I never wanted to use that, and I thought it was more useful to get to work right away. I was the head of a minority government. I knew it had a lot of constraints. I was deeply touched by the people who had been killed and wounded, and I did not want to provoke controversy with the Anglophone community, which made me not use it. I did not exploit this event for my own purposes, but I can tell you that I could have done it. It was my choice.

NOÉMI MERCIER: This victory is the culmination of more than thirty years of political commitment and hard work to lift you up to that point. What does the view look like when you finally reach the top of the mountain?

PAULINE MAROIS: There is a very great inner peace and a great satisfaction.

NOÉMI MERCIER: Inner peace?

PAULINE MAROIS: An inner peace because...how do you say that? An inner peace because I came up with a project I believed in. There was a very well-defined program with specific projects that concerned elderly people's loss of autonomy, the electrification of transport, projects at the cultural level, at the early childhood level, at the university level. Remember that Québec was in a state of social crisis with the students who had been on the street for months, with laws that had been very oppressive toward the students, and I was thinking that I had the opportunity to appease this situation. We had made the commitment, and I trusted the team around me with what we wanted to propose. And here I speak as much of my team of political advisers as of the departmental team and the deputies. I was convinced that what we had put forward—and this is without being pretentious—was something that met the needs of the Québec population. I was thinking how fortunate I was as a woman head of state to move Québec toward greater equality, toward a greener Québec, toward a richer Québec. It was clear in my head— there were all these projects with their parts finding their place one after the other, even on the question of secularism, which caused a lot of debates. We knew where we were going. When I arrived as the head of the state, I was very serene and willing to assume this function, and I was really honestly comfortable in my skin. Had it not been because we were a minority, I think that we would have implemented many of the projects we had put forward.

NOÉMI MERCIER: A little over a month and a half later, you were fired by your constituents and then the Parti Québécois lost the election. You have experienced many hardships in your career, setbacks, painful episodes. What is your philosophy in the face of failure? How do you deal with that?

PAULINE MAROIS: I am exceptionally lucky to not be a woman of bitterness. I am positive and able to see, even in defeat, what can be useful, what can be beautiful, what can be good. But honestly, I did not see much then. My defeat in 2014 is still hurting. It's been hurting for a long time. It's true that I am beginning to be more serene vis-à-vis all that I have lived through. In fact, again, it is to [decide] not to go to the end of commitments that I had not taken to be at the height of what the Québec citizens were expecting of a female premier.

NOÉMI MERCIER: Ah, this is the woman premier's side?

PAULINE MAROIS: On one side, a woman premier...it played a big part in my reaction to defeat. Yes, very much. I thought to myself, as a woman I had a lot to offer. I had a certain vision of equality between men and women. Measures that needed to be put in place to consolidate this perspective. Major social policies. I am a social democrat who believed in a more equal sharing of wealth. I am a woman who believes in the environment—beyond a few more specific projects, a huge one was the electrification of transport that would lead us to eliminate oil, etc. That was great.

NOÉMI MERCIER: But do you feel responsible on behalf of women?

PAULINE MAROIS: Yes, yes, among others, and I also felt that I was disappointing Quebecers as a woman. I thought it was a pity because it might take a while for another woman to be chosen.

NOÉMI MERCIER: Because of your defeat?

PAULINE MAROIS: Partly. Not only for that but partly, and the wound was very large, very important, very long to heal.

NOÉMI MERCIER: Then what?

PAULINE MAROIS: Now, I am more serene, much more serene and because I have never stopped watching what is happening in politics, I am compelled to do it. I get up in the morning, and I make my editorial comments to my husband. We laugh a lot, but that's it. I had the impression that as a woman I had a lot to offer and that I was going to disappoint people who had trusted me, but at the same time, they had to keep trusting me. It's the people who made this decision, I did not. Democracy is, I would say, so important in our collective lives, in our states, that you never question it even if it goes against what you believe.

NOÉMI MERCIER: During the last fifty years in Canada there were 111 men who were prime ministers or premiers, and they were in office for 2,060 days, on average—thus about two mandates. Twelve[6] women were prime ministers or premiers, and they were in power for 1,198 days, on average—less than [one full] mandate. How do you explain it? Are voters more demanding, less patient toward political women than male politicians at the highest levels?

PAULINE MAROIS: It's possible. Yes, it's possible. Honestly, I've been thinking a little bit about this lately, among other things, for all sorts of reasons. Nevertheless, we still have a slightly different style of leadership and although I said that I had a killer instinct, it remains that we are more conciliating, we accept being mistaken more. And it can be that we want so much, and then the population expects so much more of us because we had never been there before. We're going to be better, we're going to have better results, we want to do bigger things.

NOÉMI MERCIER: People expect more of women than men?

PAULINE MAROIS: Yes. Much like ourselves, we put more on our shoulders. I think people expect more. And we also have our

....

[6] At the time of this interview, Caroline Cochrane and Heather Stefanson had not yet been elected as first ministers.

flaws. We're not perfect, we make mistakes too, but we can make very good decisions and some bad, and maybe the expectations are disproportionate compared to what we can do, what we can give, even if we give the best of ourselves.

NOÉMI MERCIER: I am convinced of that. If you even look at your career, it's amazing how much you've had to prove yourself.

PAULINE MAROIS: All the time, once, twice, three, four times before you're trusted.

NOÉMI MERCIER: It took three attempts before you became head of the PQ.

PAULINE MAROIS: That's right.

NOÉMI MERCIER: When you became the leader, some in your caucus rebelled.

PAULINE MAROIS: That's right. Absolutely.

NOÉMI MERCIER: Then, when you got elected, you were voted in as a minority.

PAULINE MAROIS: Exactly. And unfortunately, following internal divisions within our party, that brought about a party that preyed on some of our voters.

NOÉMI MERCIER: Option Nationale?

PAULINE MAROIS: Option Nationale, not to name it.

NOÉMI MERCIER: Can we talk either about Quebecers or your own colleagues who had more trouble seeing you, a woman, in the role of leader, [and] to accept you as a leader?

PAULINE MAROIS: I think there is something there somewhere. It may be in the subconscious, it is not conscious, but I think so. I think so. There is more to be said to have a man "boss," a man leader, a man premier with the people around us, with our colleagues, than a woman. There is no model. We have a few European models, but there is not really a model in any meaningful way.

NOÉMI MERCIER: It cannot be said that there are 20, 30, 40 per cent of women heads of state around the world because every time there is one we look at her in a way.... We scan her.

PAULINE MAROIS: Absolutely, I'm watching Jacinda Ardern, she's the prime minister of New Zealand. Mme Dardenne. But yes, Mrs. Merkel, who left to not be defeated: I find it wise of her. Despite everything she did some interesting things. You can love or not love her. No matter what model you have.

NOÉMI MERCIER: The question is, how do we encourage more women to be interested in politics—because of many girls and women who want to change the world—they do not perceive themselves naturally in the role of politician.

PAULINE MAROIS: I tell them two things: think you can change the life of your grandson if you have little children and want to present yourself in politics and offer alternatives in terms of social policies; think that you can change your grandmother's life, that you can adopt support policies, and that you can help seniors with support and help at home; think that you can make sure your country is going to be richer because you will have made good decisions and that your citizens are going to be happier; think of the good you can do. All the ideas you have are good and they can be useful to correct injustices that shock you, that challenge you, and then you are ready. Trust yourself. Stop doubting your talents, your abilities. Go over the doubts even if sometimes you have to keep some, but not too many. Then, as a society, that is what women can do.

NOÉMI MERCIER: That's right, you're right. We need to learn to trust each other. But as a society, as a political party, as a system of education, what should we do? First, there are so many things that have also been done in our systems. I think of "Chapeau, les filles" [Hats off, girls!]—it was a great program to value non-traditional trades. There is a lot of work that is done by the council on the status of women by different ministries.

PAULINE MAROIS: But the work-family reconciliation policies often affect women more. I think that the CPE policy has had more impact, [and] the early childhood centres and the reduced-price childcare services have had more impact on equality between men and women than a multitude of other policies. [Now,] women, heads of single-parent households, can return to school, to work, knowing that their children would be safe, and especially [knowing] they were going to have an income. Women's employment rates in Québec have increased in the labour market. It is the highest in Canada. In Québec, I learned—Pierre Fortin told me last week, because we were at the same event—"We have the highest rate of women's labour market activity for women of childbearing age." And around the world....

NOÉMI MERCIER: In the world?

PAULINE MAROIS: Yes, I had forgotten to add "in the world." The highest rate of activity of women of childbearing age and there-fore the highest rate of activity of women of childbearing age in Québec is the highest in the world....

NOÉMI MERCIER: And this, we owe you, Mme. Marois.

PAULINE MAROIS: In part, Lucien Bouchard helped a little as premier....

NOÉMI MERCIER: And all that when you look at all the hardships you have overcome, the humiliation, the failures....

PAULINE MAROIS: Yes.

NOÉMI MERCIER: Was it worth it?

PAULINE MAROIS: Yes. I would take the same course—corrected some small errors here and there, but I would take the same course. Lately, I walk around the streets and all the young people accost me regularly. I participated in a TV show, radio, I received a lot of emails saying, "Mrs. Marois, you changed my life." Just for those ten emails that I had…in connection with the CPE. And if we go back, I could tell you about all the projects that were put in place to allow women to return to school when they were single mothers when I was minister of labour and security of the revenue. We have secularized the schools, which helped francization in Québec. In the end, there were many things, but for the CPE, I have to say that I think it was worth it, really.

Translation courtesy of Canada 2020 *No Second Chances* podcast.

RACHEL NOTLEY

PREMIER OF ALBERTA
(2015-2019)

When I began conducting *No Second Chances* interviews, I can remember thinking to myself that there was no way Rachel Notley was going to agree to be part of this project. At the time, Notley was the only serving female first minister in the country. She'd led the Alberta New Democratic Party to a somewhat surprising victory in 2015, defeating a forty-four–year Progressive Conservative streak and the longest-standing provincial government in Canadian history. She'd now almost completed her first term and was in the throes of a re-election campaign (and quite a difficult one at that). She was literally seeking a second chance.

As anticipated, Notley's team politely declined our offer—and understandably so, given that the request was coming from an out-of-province political scientist working on a podcast banging the drum about Canadians not re-electing female first ministers.

The election came and went. The Alberta NDP lost to Jason Kenney's United Conservative Party. Among other reasons, I quietly mourned another case study for the project. When the dust settled in Alberta, I received a note from Notley's team. She was ready to participate in an interview if we were still interested. I hopped on a plane for Edmonton.

Rachel Notley was born with New Democrat roots in a very political world. She grew up in the town of Fairview in northern Alberta, the oldest of three children raised by her mother, Sandra, and father, Grant Notley. When Rachel Notley was four years old, her father became the leader of Alberta's New Democratic Party (NDP), a post he held throughout her childhood. Notley wasn't even ten years old the first time she went out protesting with her mother. "She took me on some anti-war demonstration. I honestly can't even remember what is was," said Notley in a *Maclean's* interview in 2015. "I remember walking across the High Level Bridge and thinking, 'Wow, this is really a very long walk.'"

In Notley's second year of university, her father was tragically killed in a plane crash in northern Alberta. Notley went on to finish her studies and then ultimately follow in his footsteps. She was first elected to Alberta's provincial legislative assembly as a member of the NDP in 2008 and was subsequently re-elected in 2012 with the highest vote share of any candidate in Alberta that year. In 2015, Notley led the party to a historic victory and became the seventeenth premier of Alberta.

I'm not sure what I was expecting when I knocked on Notley's front door. Until very recently, she had been the premier and had continued to serve as the MLA (member of the legislative assembly) for Edmonton-Strathcona as well as the leader of the Alberta New Democratic Party. But I recall thinking that Notley's home was more normal than I expected. It had the energy of children and pets and working parents. The newspaper was spread on the table amid homework books and a half-finished breakfast. Notley welcomed me in warmly and poured me a cup of coffee quickly and efficiently; someone used to jam-packed days. If I had imagined that post-premiership life was relaxing, this was not what I saw in Rachel Notley. She continued tidying the kitchen and making the odd call or email check as we got acquainted and I set up our recording equipment. At one point during the interview, she had to pause for a short media interview. She stepped out to her front porch, asking if I could keep an eye on the dog in her absence.

I can remember thinking, Rachel Notley and politics are far from over. I so hope that a historic second chance is still to come.

"You can do the same case over and over and over and even be very successful at it—or you can just change the damn law so stupid things stop happening." Rachel Notley followed her late father as leader of the NDP in Alberta, eventually becoming premier.

RACHEL NOTLEY: I was born in Edmonton. I often tell people that I think I was almost a month old before my dad met me, because he was off managing a campaign in Saskatchewan when I was born. He was the provincial secretary for the Alberta NDP. I guess it's fair to say that politics has been there from day one. I'm looking over your shoulder right now at some old family pictures on the wall. They're lovely, of our family when we were kids, but they're all leftover pictures from when we hired professional photographers to take photos for campaign leaflets and stuff....

We moved about six hours north of Edmonton when my dad ended up winning a riding in the very northwest part of Alberta by just fifty votes. From the time I was seven, I lived in this rural community, Fairview, with about two thousand people. And then, when I was eleven or twelve, we moved from town to an acreage overlooking the Peace River Valley. For all intents and purposes, we lived in the country. My dad was away most of the time. He'd come home two to three times a month—and when he was home, I'd be watching him run around responding to constituents' concerns. Literally, he'd get a call late at night and rush off to help some-body fix their fence because the department of transportation had knocked it down and their cattle were running free and all that kind of stuff. I definitely saw public service through those eyes. And even though he was, through almost all of his career, only one person in our party standing up against a seemingly all-powerful Progressive Conservative party—I also saw the integrity with which he worked and the degree to which the idea of standing up for democratic socialist values drove him. When I was very young—about five—my mom described what my dad did by telling me the story of Robin Hood and just basically saying, your dad is Robin Hood. He wants people with less to be able to get their fair share, and he doesn't want them to be taken to the cleaners by people who have more power and more money. So that's what I was raised with. My mom was not an elected politician, but she was certainly also a social justice activist. It permeated everything that she did as well. So, the long and the short of it is between my dad and my mom I was raised in a household that valued activism, valued social justice activism, and defined the act of doing everything you can to make life better for people who didn't otherwise have a voice as being the noble thing—that you didn't measure the decision to try against the likelihood of success. You just understood that the decision to try was the right decision.

KATE GRAHAM: Do you ever recall as a kid thinking, 'Maybe someday I'm going to do that?'

RACHEL NOTLEY: You know, for the most part I didn't. I thought that what I would do was become a lawyer. I went to school at Osgoode [Hall Law School], and I went to school with a lot of folks whose main focus was to get that job on Bay Street. My main focus was to set up a poverty law clinic and be paid in chickens. What I thought I was going to do was to be that lawyer who would stand up for folks who couldn't otherwise get access to justice, and so I wanted to be an activist, but I didn't necessarily see myself being a politician at the outset. That changed in my twenties.

KATE GRAHAM: What changed?

RACHEL NOTLEY: I think it was two things. Of course, you know my dad died in a very tragic and public accident. I was twenty-one at the time and it took almost no time for people to start coming up to me saying, "When are you gonna get involved? When are you going to do something?" Almost from day one there was this sort of pressure amongst New Democrats for me to consider running and to get involved electorally. I mostly dismissed it. Then I got the opportunity to work in politics both during the latter part of my university years and after I became a lawyer. That gave me an opportunity to see, first of all, that it's fun and, secondly, that you have the potential to make much more change much more quickly in politics if you actually get into a position of power. And so, I had the opportunity to go out to BC where there was an NDP government and work with the attorney general. In those twelve months, we brought in the first regime of laws outside of Québec to protect same-sex couples and their rights to start a family together. We pushed it through the premier's office—it didn't happen right away, we had to push—and then my minister and I had to go 'round and sell it.

Ultimately, we showed that you could make the right arguments and sell it. So, you see this high level of agency that you can have in politics. I was doing labour law, and workers' rights and poverty law to some degree. I quickly learned that you can do the same case over and over and over and over, and even be successful at it—or you can just change the darn law so stupid things stop happening. It's that really concentrated agency that comes from achieving political power.

KATE GRAHAM: I gather this brings us to about 2004, with lots of speculation that you might run. Can you tell me a little bit about what that decision-making process looked like for you?

RACHEL NOTLEY: When we moved back to Alberta from BC, my husband and I started talking about how I might run. Our kids were one and three. We knew I would likely run in the area that we had moved to; it had been my home and it's the place I identify as home. It was just a question of when. There was a very popular NDP MLA, one of two in the province who already held the seat, so to some degree the timing was defined by how long he was going to stay. And honestly, if he had agreed to stay on another four years, it probably would have been better for me. I would have been just as happy so that my kids could have been a bit older. But he decided to step down, and I knew that that was the opportunity to win the nomination.

Because I grew up in politics, I believed I could do the job of being an MLA while still being present for my kids. And I think that was true. We thought it was going to be a hotly contested nomination. I started quietly—and then not so quietly—campaigning for it, and nobody ended up running against me.

KATE GRAHAM: Did you ever imagine at that time that this was the beginning of a path to the premiership?

RACHEL NOTLEY: Absolutely not! I did not think that was in the plan. I thought it was an opportunity to make some changes through advocacy as an opposition member and I thought it was an opportunity to build the future of the NDP in Alberta so that we would have more influence. I honestly did not think about leading it nor did I think about becoming premier at that point.

KATE GRAHAM: A lot of women say no to running for office, but even fewer women take the leap to run for leader. Walk me through that.

RACHEL NOTLEY: That was a much harder decision to make, actually. It was not as easy because I did know how much more of a job that was. And I knew that it was not only time-consuming, but that the buck always stops with you, that the future of the party was on your shoulders, that the effectiveness of the caucus was on your shoulders. And that, frankly, the day could never end when you're the leader if you do the job well enough and you care enough about it. There's no reason for you not to be working twenty-three out of every twenty-four hours, seven days a week. How do you do that while balancing things with your kids and your family? So, it was a much tougher decision. There were a lot of people who really pressured me over the course of about eighteen months. I started with a definite no, slowly moved to a maybe, and then eventually a yes, but it wasn't an easy decision. When I finally gave it serious consideration, I had a long conversation with my kids to see if they were okay with it. And they said they were, although I think it's fair to say that when I subsequently became premier a mere eight months after I became leader, they'd had no idea what they were saying yes to. My husband was one of the people pressuring me to run. So, yes, it was a tough decision, but ultimately things were really volatile in Alberta, and I could run and probably give it the best result it ever would have. Then there would be enough other people in play that I could step back and pass it on to someone to take it to the next stage. This was 2014. No one was expecting we were going to be doing a run for government. We ended up being a lot more successful than we expected.

KATE GRAHAM: So now you're the leader. You're in election mode. You're still an MLA but you have this enormous additional thing you've taken on. What was that period like for you prior to the election?

RACHEL NOTLEY: It was pretty insane. I got elected on October 18, 2014. The next day was the anniversary of my dad's plane crash. Being at the thirty-year memorial for my dad the day after I'd become the leader…. There was a massive group of people there and it was historic and meaningful. But I really jumped in. The next election was supposed to be in the spring of 2016, so we thought, 'We've got a year and a half, so we can slowly and methodically do the work to get the party ready.' When I was elected, we were already about a week into four by-elections that Premier [Jim] Prentice had called. We had to rush headlong into them. We made a breakthrough in Edmonton. We didn't win but we bumped up our percentage substantially in an unexpected area. It was a modest gain. Premier Prentice give a speech the next morning. I remember speaking to the provincial secretary of our party at that point, saying, "Listen, that guy is not going to wait till 2016. He's going to call the election in the next six months. Just watch…."

We'd all been so tired, dragging our way through our own leadership race and dealing with the by-elections. We were a very small party at that point. We just had to jump right into it and start looking for candidates and fundraising and doing all that work. When you're a caucus of four, to be ready for an election where there's eighty-seven candidates in a province-wide campaign, and where the other guys are going to spend—I think they spent between five and ten million dollars, and I think we had about fifty thousand dollars in our bank account—it was ridiculous. I can barely remember it, because we worked so hard every day just trying to get everything in place. But we had some good signs along the way. People became more interested in talking to us and we got some good candidates. That was very exciting. We managed to pull people into our campaign; some from out of province who normally wouldn't have cared because the NDP dismissed Alberta as being a particularly relevant player in progressive politics….

Two months before the election, we became more optimistic. Even though we were working 24/7, we were starting to tick up. I remember thinking, 'We're going to be official opposition—this is pretty cool. I think we might actually hit fifteen seats.' We were all having a great old time. It was a fun campaign because everything looked like we were going to do much better than we ever had before. We were the little engine that could. Obviously when you go from being at 10 per cent in the polls to 40 per cent, the road is mostly filled with good news. It allowed us to get through exceptionally long days.

KATE GRAHAM: I've heard a story about you in the hotel room right before the election, getting the news about how the party was doing in the polls. People started to predict that you were going to win. Obviously, it's great for your party, but for you personally, it also meant something very significant....

RACHEL NOTLEY: Oh, it was horrifying. Oh, yeah. We had a hardworking crew of about eight people in our caucus before the campaign started, and myself and three other employees who had been in the legislature, and now we're taking over the government. I mean, we just weren't sure how we were going to be able to manage the levers of power with such a small team given the complexity and the depth of the issues that we had to address. We had elected fifty great MLAs but most with little experience. They were really smart people and wonderful humans, but not people who had signed up—in many cases—to be MLAs let alone ministers. It was quite overwhelming. There was a point when I looked at how Alison Redford had left office, and what that was like for her, that I thought to myself, 'Good Lord, please don't let me be driven out of this office on the end of a pointy stick the way she was.' As it turned out, we managed to scramble up the learning cliff and ultimately establish a record that I'm very proud of.

KATE GRAHAM: As the second female premier of the province, did gender factor into the campaign or how you were treated by the media?

RACHEL NOTLEY: That night in October when I sat down with a provincial secretary and said, "Oh, my Lord, we have six months to put together a campaign and we have to find eighty-seven candidates." I said, "Let me be very clear: we will run forty-four or more candidates who are women and don't even think of coming to me with a roster of candidates who do not fit that description." I was emphatic about that. When appointing my cabinet, I said the same thing. "This Cabinet will consist of 50 per cent women. That is all there is to it." We created the first ever ministry of women's affairs in the province. When I expanded my cabinet, I remember everyone speculating about who I would put in. "Well, you couldn't possibly put in this person because she's seven months pregnant." But then at the swearing-in, there she is. Seven months pregnant, getting sworn into Cabinet. And, oh, by the way, the other woman being sworn in? She's three months pregnant, too. Because guess what? Albertans get pregnant and therefore it's not unreasonable that periodically people of that description will find themselves leading the province. We made that a priority. We introduced a gender-based analysis, making sure that many policies were considered through this lens. We weren't perfect, but we were intentional about trying to do it as much as we could.

KATE GRAHAM: What about you, personally?

RACHEL NOTLEY: There are many factors about how politics is done that make it harder for women to be politicians. It's hard to say how much of it was because I was a woman and how much of it was because I was a New Democrat trying to make significant, progressive change while Alberta was going through an unprecedented economic recession. The people who were most overt at critiquing me tended to be men and tended to be on the right of the spectrum. As a result, their criticism was more violent, using more threatening or disrespectful language. Now was that because I was a woman? Or was it about the nature of the opposition, or the nature of the challenges and struggles the province was suffering? It's hard to say, but my own experiences day to day when I was premier—even during the toughest times—women consistently and regularly came to me and said, "Don't listen to what they're saying. You're doing a great job. You make me so proud."

KATE GRAHAM: This is a slight departure here, but there were big changes happening in the landscape with conservative parties in Alberta at the same time. There were two women in the race and they both end up stepping out. What was your observation about gender in what was happening within the broader political landscape?

RACHEL NOTLEY: Well, I think there are common characteristics or features in politics that are nonpartisan in nature but that put up barriers to women. There are also features of political activity that are, in fact, partisan in nature, where some parties put up more barriers than others. I'd said we weren't running a team of politicians who weren't 50 per cent women, as an example. What happened with the UCP—I mean it was horrible to see the treatment that both Donna Kennedy-Glans and Sandra Jansen were subjected to. Under no circumstances would that ever have happened in our party. If that convention had happened somehow as part of an NDP convention, the whole bloody thing would have derailed. The remainder of the members would have wanted to take the fifteen or twenty people who harassed, in particular Sandra Jansen, and stop the convention, eject them from the party, and condemn their behaviour. That's what would have happened. There is no way on the planet that kind of behaviour would have been allowed, that the women would have been cast aside like that and called a robust democracy or whatever it was that Jason Kenney called it at the time. It was very disappointing.

KATE GRAHAM: Indeed. Let's get back to your story. Tell me about being premier.

RACHEL NOTLEY: I believed that we needed to be aggressive and active. On combating climate change, our plan in Alberta led to the federal government being able to do what they did, in terms of going to Paris and making the commitments that they did. Ultimately, the carbon levy and the carbon tax were used against us by the opposition, but I still think they were the right decisions. They demonstrated how you can make progress on combating climate change and still maintain economic sustainability. The decision to reject it was political. It wasn't economic. There was no negative drag on Alberta's economic prospects because of the plan. We also did great stuff on workers' rights, leading the country on the minimum wage. We cut the rate of child poverty in half in Alberta during what was the most difficult economic period the province had been through in decades. We introduced legislation around the protection of LGBTQ kids in schools and also developed policy that allowed us to go to all schools and say, "Listen, if you're getting a dollar of public money, you're going to live by these rules of inclusion and respect and equality. If you don't want to do it, have at 'er, but you're not getting any more public money." I'm very proud of that.

KATE GRAHAM: Let's talk about the lead up to the 2019 election.

RACHEL NOTLEY: It was frustrating in many respects. Probably the most critical challenge that we wrestled with was job creation and supporting Alberta's energy industry so we could continue to bring jobs back, as we did. I mean, at one point, we'd lost 150,000 jobs in this province, probably more. We were also in a position where, frankly, the state of Alberta's energy industry was dragging down economic prosperity for the rest of the country, and that was not going to change if we didn't get a handle on it. We worked and were able to win the federal government–approved Trans Mountain pipeline. That was some hard-nosed negotiating, but we saw the economy ticking up and jobs being created and people's sense of optimism was really growing. I wish we had called the election then. But then the pipeline decision was overturned and we had to go back to the books on that. The issue became symbolic of our economic health and people's ability to get jobs and take care of their families. It became a stand-in for that. And so, when that decision was delayed in late August 2018, we weren't able to ship our product. The world was paying fifty dollars a barrel for oil, and Canadians were getting eight dollars a barrel because we had no way to move the product. The economy slowed, and people got very anxious. It was a hard time for us, we'd committed to calling the election in the spring but we knew that the sense of optimism we so needed Albertans to have had shifted again. I think we made the right moves, and we saved a lot of jobs, and we created a lot too. It still wasn't enough. We knew we were going to be the people that most folks looked to blame. That's what you do when you worry about making your mortgage payments, right? You blame the folks who are in charge.

KATE GRAHAM: Do you think your gender was a part of this story?

RACHEL NOTLEY: I think it's harder for women in politics, so I will not ever be the one that says, "Oh, gender is not an issue." But the fact that I am a woman was probably not the driving issue for what happened to my party. I don't know really that it was because I was a woman. I will say because of what was going on with Alberta's politics, people really wanted a fighter and someone who was tough. It is possible that because I'm a woman people didn't see me as being tough enough, but there are other times in my career where people have, in fact, defined me as being a tough fighter; if anything, my gender is a plus in a way because it's put on its head.

KATE GRAHAM: So how do we make sense of the fact that no woman in Canada has gone through what you just did—a second general election campaign as premier and leader—and won?

RACHEL NOTLEY: I think there's more than one factor going on there. One thing we're seeing across the board in politics right now is that few governments are lasting more than one term. When I started going to the Council of the Federation, I think there was one premier who was there from when I first got elected. Every other premier has lost their job, male or female. Some people have talked about, you know, the Amazon phenomenon. People who don't like their government just want to click and order a new one. And there are certain features to politics that make it harder for women. We know women are caregivers in the family. They do more work at home. And politics requires you to be available at long and unpredictable hours away from home. It requires you to put yourself into the public eye and just cross your fingers that there's no blowback against you or the people you love. It's a very unpredictable line of work. And politics is aggressive. People fight with you, and that's across left and right. I think women are either pushed out or they choose not to seek positions of leadership because that's not the way they want to do things. We need to think about how we can change that.

KATE GRAHAM: Today, as I sit here in your kitchen, there are no women at that table. What do you think is the impact of that?

RACHEL NOTLEY: It's really, really unfortunate because there is a difference between men and women in terms of the public policy initiatives that they put forward. I mean, that's actually a thing. We said in the last election that we were going to bring in full, twenty-five-dollar-a-day, high-quality childcare to anybody who needed it across the province. That's not a thing that I believe a male premier will go to bat for and yet it's so important. The research is incontrovertible that women continue to bear the majority of the work when it comes to the family in Canada. And that will always draw from their ability to ascend to leadership positions in other parts of society. Moreover, I think that right now, apart from Andrea Horwath and me—and my apologies to any woman whom I'm missing on the provincial level—but I don't know if there's another female official opposition leader who's even waiting in the wings. This all-male bachelor episode is not going to end anytime soon.

KATE GRAHAM: For women who are thinking about getting into politics, watching what happened here may be disheartening. What would you say to them?

RACHEL NOTLEY: It goes back to what I was talking about at the very beginning. If you believe in something and you think that it's going to make a real difference in the lives of people, just focus on fighting for it and working for it. Don't get so far ahead of yourself that you paralyze yourself from taking action. That doesn't mean you can't be strategic about getting to that end goal, but at the same time, don't let that stop you from taking the first step. The ability of women to take their rightful place in leadership positions depends in part on women demanding their rightful place, even when it looks like they're up against long odds.

KATE GRAHAM: Having now gone through this whole experience, if you could go back to the beginning, would you do it all again?

RACHEL NOTLEY: Oh yeah. I mean, sometimes when I'm talking to a friend I went to law school with and they're enjoying their third vacation in Europe that year, I think, 'Oh God, why did I make such bad life choices?' [laughs] But then there are moments, even in the time since the election, that I'm suddenly overwhelmed thinking about what we did. I know some of these achievements will make me very proud for the rest of my life....

For years and years and years, people have been talking about the need to get women involved in politics and there is a school of thought that all you need to do is reach out and be more encouraging. Quite frankly, that's what we've been doing for decades and we haven't really moved the dial. We need to look very hard at the kinds of things that bar women from participating—and not just women politicians but giving all women a fair platform from which to start their work in any kind of leadership position in society. I'm a huge advocate for public childcare and I'm not ever going to stop talking about it. I honestly think that if we had high-quality, low-cost, affordable, public childcare, about ten years later you would see the number of women involved in politics shoot up in an incredible way. We need to find ways to make politics more family friendly. We should call people out for bullying. I think that parties ultimately have to make a commitment, too. We are not going to have 50 per cent elected women if we don't have 50 per cent women running and it's the parties that make that decision. There is a 30 per cent differential between what men and women earn. There is a huge differential in the amount of days, the amount of hours and days, that women and men work—whether it's paid or not paid—and you're not going to get an equal number of women coming forward unless you create the system that requires an equal number of women to come forward. So, that's what I think. Make the changes and soon enough you won't have to make it a requirement anymore. It'll just happen.

ALISON REDFORD

PREMIER OF ALBERTA
(2011-2014)

When I asked Alison Redford what it was like being Alberta's first female premier, she responded with a laugh and two curious words: "Grey suits."

"When you look in my closet, you can see the clothes I wore when I was premier. Grey suits, button-down shirts with French cuffs, loafers. If I wore a dress, it was attached to a suit. Without even realizing it, the message I sent and the message that was received was, 'Yeah, she's a woman. But look at her! She looks like a man. She dresses like a man.'"

We went upstairs and she showed me her closet—she wasn't kidding. In a closet that includes lots of colour and a range of cloth-ing pieces, there stands a section—the "being premier" section—of almost exclusively grey suits.

Alison Redford was born in British Columbia but grew up in Calgary, Alberta. She completed a law degree at the University of Saskatchewan and worked on constitutional and legal reform cases both in Canada and internationally. She was one of only four com-missioners appointed by the secretary-general of the United Nations to administer Afghanistan's first parliamentary election. She served as an advisor to the Privy Council Office and worked on assign-ments in Serbia, Namibia, Uganda, Zimbabwe, Mozambique, the Philippines, and Vietnam. She also worked as an advisor to two Canadian prime ministers, Joe Clark and Brian Mulroney.

Redford entered politics in 2008, winning a seat as the Progressive Conservative candidate in the provincial riding of Calgary-Elbow. She was appointed to Cabinet as the minister of justice and attorney general. After Premier Ed Stelmach announced plans to retire, Redford sought the leadership. While not considered a frontrunner, she won, making her the first female premier of Alberta. In 2012, she led the party to a majority victory—but this was short-lived. A series of contentious issues dogged Redford until she resigned in 2014.

I'd read a bit about the controversies before meeting Redford at her home in Calgary. I knew about the travel expenses and taking her child with her on a few international trips, sparking a lot of curiosity about motherhood and politics and the extent to which the unfamiliarity between the two played a role in the political demise of Alison Redford. As a lawyer and as someone who had spent a career pursuing democratic renewal around the world, it seemed unlikely to me that what I was reading online really captured the story.

And so, I sat at Redford's dining room table. We laughed and we cried, and I listened to how raw the wounds of a life in politics can be, even years after the fact. It was a glimpse into the personal impact of the frailties of a political system where there are no second chances for those who break the mould. Our conversation left me wondering whether it is our leaders who fail us or whether we fail them.

"The foundation of what makes communities great is the power of the vote." Alison Redford was Alberta's first woman premier.

ALISON REDFORD: My dad worked in the oil patch as an electrician, and so we travelled around the world. I grew up in Borneo for six years when I was young; I didn't come back to Canada until I was about twelve. I was very close to my maternal grandfather, who was known for helping people. He had worked in the mines in Scotland. He and my granny immigrated in 1948. My granny had worked in a candy factory from when she was fourteen years old. She was the oldest of thirteen kids and it was sort of like the Catherine Cookson novel, you know? Her teacher came to the house and said, "You know, we'd really like her to be a teacher." And my great-grandpa said, "No, she's got to go to work. We have to support the family." She went and worked in a candy factory until she was twenty-four and married my grandpa. They had four kids, and the oldest one actually died of a respiratory illness in Glasgow. Probably because of pollution where they lived. They decided to immigrate here. They moved to Edmonton and my grandpa worked hard all his life; giving back to the community was really important to him. I remember, even as a kid, he used to buy houses in Redwater and he would renovate them because he liked to, and then he'd sell them to people in the community not at a profit; just because they needed a house, and he'd finance the deal. I mean he wasn't a wealthy person, but he would make sure that, you know, families that had lots of kids and needed a place to live had one. So, I remember from a very young age learning that you had to have compassion for people, that people very often ended up in situations that had nothing to do with their own doing. It's simply circumstances that there are people in the world who are vulnerable and the rest of us have an obligation to help. And it doesn't come from anything other than wanting to treat people the way you would hope you'd be treated, or the people that you cared about and loved would be treated if something terrible happened to them....

I lived in different places when I was a kid. I didn't see desperate poverty, but I certainly saw people who didn't have the sort of material possessions that we would be used to or were used to in the 1970s in North America. I was always aware that there were vulnerable people, and that it was important to take care of vulnerable people because we were blessed to have what we did. That was my ethos in everything I did. I was very aware when people weren't nice to people. That bothered me a lot. For me, politics was always about watching people in the community who did good things to help the community. I've always thought of politics and government as being about trying to make community and society better.

KATE GRAHAM: You moved around a lot as a kid and then your early career also took you all over the world. It was a pretty short time between coming back to Canada and formally stepping into politics. Can you tell me about that first decision to say, "All right, I'm going to run?"

ALISON REDFORD: My sister told me something I had not realized until after I'd finished in politics and started to think about where I wanted to work. It always seemed to be somewhere else. I said, "Isn't that strange?" And she said, "Well, no, it's not, Alison, because actually, except for the time that you were a politician in Canada, you never worked in Canada." I worked a little bit in Ottawa for Joe Clark and Brian Mulroney. But I always seemed to gravitate to somewhere else. Even when I came back to Canada, I was ready to settle down and practice law and very quickly ended up working on international projects....

I was working in Afghanistan for the Electoral Commission for the 2005 parliamentary elections, which were their first parliamentary elections. And I was one of the commissioners but, because I was the woman, I was doing a lot of work educating women in communities. Once we went to Helmand province but ended up getting delayed because of some security issue. I walked into the school three hours late, and there must have been sixty women in burqas sitting there with their daughters waiting for me. That was a really important and very brave step for them because they were targets sitting in a building for three hours when everyone knew they were sitting there to learn about how to vote for the first time in their lives. And they sat there. It was experiences like that. I realized that, even though I'd been involved in public policy, and I've been involved in community work, the most important and the most fundamental model—the foundation for what makes communities great—is the power of the vote. As an elected person, you are representing everyone who voted for you. And that it doesn't matter if you're the chief of staff to the prime minister or if you're the latest chief of staff in the White House, the person who ultimately is responsible and accountable and has the right to speak is the person who's elected.

I watched what was happening in my own province. It was a terrible time there and in Alberta from my perspective, because I'm very much on the left side of the spectrum, very much the progressive in Progressive Conservative. There had been so many times where I felt that previous governments had made really bad choices that weren't respectful, that didn't accommodate vulnerable people. They used wedge issues and created narratives of intolerance to get elected, and it brought out conflict as opposed to compromise to try to win. I didn't like that....

I just decided I'd had enough. I was now a mom—Sarah was three years old. I ran for a nomination for the federal Progressive Conservative Party first. I didn't win, but people were surprised by how close it was. And then I decided to run when Ralph Klein stepped down. That was the riding I lived in. I got in touch with the people who organized the nomination, who were people I've known over the course of my life. And they said, "Oh, that's great!" There was a four- or five-month window when they could have picked dates to have the nomination. I said to them, "The only time I can't do it is these two weeks because I have a family commitment I booked a year ago." And that's when they set the nomination for. So, clearly, they didn't want me to run. That was the beginning.

KATE GRAHAM: So, what did you do?

ALISON REDFORD: I didn't run for the nomination that time. They nominated someone else, and he lost spectacularly. All their best-laid plans didn't work. And then it came up again in the next election, and I thought, 'Well, I'm going to run.' There were a lot of things going on in the economy in Alberta at the time that troubled me. There was this big split between Calgary and Edmonton. And there was this sense that Edmonton, where the capital is, was where government was directed from. No one seemed to be able to facilitate a dialogue on a lot of policy issues around energy policy and royalty frameworks. Even though that wasn't my area of expertise, I felt like there was a role for someone to come in and try to bring people to the table, to try to understand each other and see what was going on. I saw a lot of complacency. A lot of politicians were pretty cynical about manipulating messages and issues and fermenting intolerance and anger, and I just didn't want it. I knew that I didn't want my daughter growing up in a place like that. And if I had a shot at trying to stop and change that, I wanted to be part of it. It was important to me to draw a line in the sand and say, "We have to change this conversation because we're not even talking about the right things anymore." So, I decided to run.

KATE GRAHAM: Tell me about that campaign and your early days of becoming an MLA [member of the legislative assembly]. What stands out in your mind when you think back to that time?

ALISON REDFORD: As a society, we look for people who can be a voice for us and will participate in a process for us. It was interesting to evolve into one of those people. I had worked for people like that, and I had worked with people like that, and I had worked to get people elected, but I had never been the candidate. I'd never been the elected member. And I absolutely loved it. Door knocking was not something I'd ever done. I'm very shy, I was never the centre of attention. The first time you walk up to a door and say, "Hi, my name's Alison Redford and I'd like to be your MLA," you have no idea what the person on the other side of that door is going to say. I would door knock seven, eight hours a day. It was incredible how it became like the frog in the boiling water. You don't realize that you're starting to play a different role in terms of how you talk to people, how you listen to people, how you start to connect what different people are saying. You also learn what really resonates with you. What impacted me the most was, by the time I was elected as the MLA, I had a sense of this riding that was entirely different from anything I'd thought of when I'd started six months before.

I was elected. There's this quiet period, you know, your campaign goes out and takes down your campaign signs and someone from the legislature calls and says, "Okay, we need this paperwork."

And you hear nothing. I went about my business and took my dogs for a walk and went grocery shopping. I was watching the news and people were starting to speculate that I might be in Cabinet because I was elected, and I was a woman, and I was a lawyer. It really was neither here nor there to me, I was just happy to be elected, and then about four days later I got a call from the premier asking me to be the justice minister. That accelerated things. "Now, we need you tomorrow...."

I was justice minister. I served as provincial secretary and was involved in the protocol of swearing in the cabinet and things like that. I was thrown into an official ceremonial role as well as being a new MLA. It just got really, really busy after that. I'll say this, and people will hear me say it and they'll think, "Well that's ridiculous, you should have known that." If I was listening, I'd say, "Well, of course it's like that." But I will tell you that until you've gone through it, you have no idea even at that level of being an MLA or being a minister, the impact it has on your life when you've never had that before. There's not such a thing as a day off. And that's not a complaint, it's just a reality. You don't wake up in the morning, put on your suit, go to the office at eight o'clock and leave at five o'clock at night. When I went to Safeway, I would end up having a conversation about, you know, Chinese investment in Nexen because that's where I would meet people who wanted to talk about it. And I loved it. But it's an incredible adjustment in terms of the pace of your life.

KATE GRAHAM: How did your family and daughter manage these transitions from candidate to MLA to cabinet minister? Those are big jumps. How did your family feel this shift?

ALISON REDFORD: I wasn't here a lot. As you see now, our home is right across the street from Sarah's school. You know, we've had the same family friends since the time she started school. We decided I would commute or travel to where I needed for my work, whether it was Edmonton or Fredericton or Fort McMurray or Lethbridge, and our base would be in Calgary. So everything at home stayed as much the same as it possibly could, and that's always been our mantra. Sarah's world was consistent, and that was the most important thing, that we were creating a constancy and a permanency and a certainty in her life. It's like the duck paddling under the water. The feet are going crazy, but they look completely calm up top....

I wasn't here a lot of the time, but we had lots of help. My sister is close. My mum was still alive then, and my mother-in-law. We had a nanny from the time Sarah was three who would come to the house three times a week and also make sure we had groceries and clean laundry. We juggled it. Sometimes I look at people in politics, particularly men but even some women, and think, 'We have all this control over the system, or theoretically we did, but every day was a juggling act. Oh, it's Saturday night and I'm supposed to be home. But the plane couldn't get out of Grand Prairie, so I'll be home at 2:00, at 2:00 tomorrow afternoon.' Something was always unpredictable.

KATE GRAHAM: Let's talk about leadership. You were a cabinet minister and then opportunity presented itself.

ALISON REDFORD: I remember the day Premier Stelmach stepped down. We were scheduled to have a cabinet meeting in Calgary. I was at McDougall Centre, which is where the government's office, the premier's office, is. Cabinet meets there. The premier didn't arrive on the plane, and someone said, "Oh, I think you better listen to the radio." And the premier was announcing that he was stepping down. It was a tough time for him, and it wasn't totally unexpected. But we didn't expect it that day. There were four or five of us who were there for the cabinet meeting and right away the speculation started. "Who's going to run?" Ted Morton was going to. I don't remember who else, who was in Cabinet. Everybody left McDougall. I went home. Ted Morton walked out the front doors of McDougall Centre and along the street. Of course, all the TV cameras were taking pictures and asking, "Is he or isn't he?" I watched it like any other citizen, thinking, 'I wonder who's going to run?' I went home and I went about the stuff I had to do. And then I got a call from a good friend of mine who was a lawyer in town, and he said, "You know, there are a few of us talking about this, and you're a long shot. But we've been talking to a couple of really new, modern organizers who aren't the traditional party organizers, and you can win this. We can raise the money. We need you to run...."

I'm embarrassed saying that now because from the very beginning they pushed every button they had to push to get me to run. "We want you. You can win." The thing is when you're a politician, male or female, you have this kind of schizophrenic personality. You've got to be humble, for sure, but at the same time, you've got to have something in you. When someone says to you, "You can make a difference," it's like, "I can make a difference!" It's part of the formula. I might have believed that I could. But if people told me that I couldn't win and I couldn't raise money, then it really didn't matter. So, all of these things came together. I'd loved being justice minister. This is going to sound vain to some people, but I was good at being justice minister. I enjoyed it. We accomplished an awful lot. We brought together disparate groups; I was able to achieve an awful lot. It had been a really good run—and I'd enjoyed it. We'd made the whole family thing work. There'd been lots of frustrations. I mean, politics is politics and all that. But it had been a really positive experience. And so, I thought, 'Maybe it's time. Maybe Alberta is ready to do what I hoped they would'—which wasn't about me, but it was about changing the discussion. It was about a Conservative leadership campaign where we were going to be able to talk about mental health, and drug addiction, and social supports, LGBTQ rights, electronic voting, modern infrastructure in cities, public transportation, climate. All those things that everybody else in the world was talking about but Alberta wasn't....

I was excited, and so were the people who signed up to work on the campaign. We were talking about things like climate change. It was the first time people talked about it in Alberta. We talked about the importance of carbon capture and storage, and investing in intellectual property, and understanding that we were going to have to have better partnerships with First Nations and really deal with pipeline issues. Nobody had ever really talked about those things before, and [here] we were, and it was fun and it was exciting.

KATE GRAHAM: So, the people around you saw you as being a different kind of leader, and potentially a different kind of premier. Was your being a woman a part of that conversation? Did you think, 'I could be the first female?'

ALISON REDFORD: I never thought that.

KATE GRAHAM: Was your gender seen to be a plus in terms of you as a different kind of candidate or was there a worry…. We're not sure if Alberta's quite ready for this yet?

ALISON REDFORD: Alberta was a very funny place then. Let's start there. When saw how my campaign was being organized, that I was a woman did play into the change narrative of the campaign. About climate, about LGBTQ rights, about public health, all of it. I could be a voice at the table that was going to talk about issues that were different from what people expected male candidates to talk about. It was going to be a different discussion because I was a woman, and I was in the race. It was almost like, "Oh. Of course, she's going to raise these issues. She's a woman." It wasn't derogatory; it was just there. What I now understand, and I didn't then, was that depending on the campaign strategy, there were times when the campaign would want to emphasize that I was a woman and times when they wouldn't. And it was really important that I was a mom. Even though my world as a mom is probably not a very traditional one, the most important thing in my life is my child. It was like the campaign wanted to try to take strategic advantage of it. They had me talk to a bunch of kids, which I love to do because I love to talk to kids, and I love to talk to eleven-year-old girls who want to be premier and ask me why I wanted to run for premier. That's so much fun. How could that not be fun? But when I look back now, I wish I had tried to make sure that, from the very beginning, I was a little more integrated around those issues. I look at the clothes I wore when I was premier. Grey suits. Brooks Brothers button-down shirts with French cuffs. Loafers. Rarely a dress. If I wore a dress it was either to a formal event or it was a dress that was attached to a suit. Without even realizing it, I was sending the message, "Yeah, she's a woman. But look at her. She looks like a man. She dresses like a man." Maybe because I never thought about it myself or maybe because I didn't really know who I was yet. I never thought about how I would describe myself. I just lived my life, and now I think it needed more explanation. I think people needed to understand better that you could be a loving mother and still balance a 40-billion-dollar budget or be a loving mother and have a climate debate with Al Gore. I think there was still that idea that you're either the fairly traditional, typical female who juggles lots of things or you're the premier. If I ever went anywhere and took Sarah with me, we would make sure that our family paid for that ticket even though there already was a seat on the plane, and I may not have seen her for three weeks. If a man takes his child on the plane, he's a good dad. It doesn't have to be a plane—I'm off about planes because there was an issue. One of the reasons that you elected me to be premier is because I was a nice person, and I was a mom, and I balanced the budget. Okay, that's fine. But now you're the premier and there are no accommodations made for the fact that you're a mom.

KATE GRAHAM: Did you feel like there was space to revolt against that?

ALISON REDFORD: I don't even think I knew I needed to. It was, "This is what I signed up for. So here we are." I think there are some things that are still quite raw for me. I'm going to be completely honest with you. I don't even know what people are going to say about all of this, but there were lots of accusations about me. The RCMP were called in to investigate things that never turned into anything because there wasn't anything there. The ethics commissioner was called.

What hurt me the most, really hurt me, was when CBC started investigating my nanny. Angelina had worked for us for years and years and years. She was a wonderful person. She also worked part-time at McDonald's. One day, a CBC journalist came down from Edmonton and went into McDonald's and told her that, because she had once been on a government plane with me and my daughter, she could be arrested; did she want to talk about how I took care of my daughter? The only time that Angelina was ever on the plane was a night when I was justice minister and I had come to

Calgary for a dinner. Our idea was, we're not going to disrupt the household during the week. I would just go back to Edmonton and life would carry on here in Calgary. My father-in-law had been in the hospital and he died that night. I left the dinner, and I came home. My husband was doing what he needed to do, and I needed to be in Edmonton the next morning. We made an arrangement that I would go back to Edmonton that night as planned, and I would take Sarah with me, and Angelina would come. So, Angelina flew on the plane that one time. It still brings tears to my eyes, that it would all come from something that personal.

KATE GRAHAM: I'm so sorry.

ALISON REDFORD: We did the best we could. There was certainly no rule against her coming and I'm not being legalistic. We did nothing wrong. And then, all those years later, to have this person accusing someone and saying they could be criminally charged, and now did she want to talk about what I was like as a mother? Why did we need to have Angelina help take care of Sarah? The underlying assumption was that I was a bad mother. And there were lots of things like that. Sarah only had security because she needed a babysitter. It was all part of that. People don't know about all those death threats because we didn't say, as female premiers do now, "Oh, there are all these threats against me." We didn't do that. We just dealt with them.

KATE GRAHAM: This gets to the heart of what this whole project is about. There's often lots of excitement when a woman is first elected and then a moment comes—and it comes much faster for female first ministers than for men, on average—where things start to fall apart. And frankly, there are men in politics who do things that are not good and they seem to be able to weather it. Why is that?

ALISON REDFORD: Because men stick up for each other. And if you want the best possible example of that, just think about the news with Gordon Campbell. I don't know what happened, but I saw on the news that the, quote, Government of Canada did an internal investigation and found there was no merit to the claim. Are you kidding me? Do you think that if that had been Kim Campbell or me that that's where it would've ended? When men make mistakes, other men come to their defense. For us, it's pretty tough to go out there when we've been through the experiences we have. If I went out tomorrow and stood up for a woman in politics who was having a hard time, the reaction would be, "Oh yeah. But remember her. Remember what they said about her?" It's not that I don't want to put myself out there. I seriously wonder if I come out and defend a woman in public life, whether that's going to help her at all.

KATE GRAHAM: When people were attacking you, especially in situations involving your daughter or you as a mother, did you feel that any women stood up for you?

ALISON REDFORD: No. But you know...if someone came forward after and said, "No, she really did," I wouldn't argue with that because it was such a blur that I lost track. When I first stepped down, people were confused about why I did it because there was a lot of internal party stuff going on. And then, all of a sudden, three days later, there's some story about some building in Edmonton where I'm theoretically going to build an apartment for my daughter. Which wasn't true and didn't turn out to be true. But it didn't matter. And then that all just ended. I didn't spend a lot of time thinking about it then. I had to deal with my life. It went on and on and on for months and months and years. It's pretty scary. You probably don't even think much about it, but consider every time you fill out a mortgage application or passport application. I travel a lot and go to countries where I fill out immigration forms. And there's always that question, whether you've ever been convicted of a criminal offence. And the number of times I've thought to myself, 'My God, you know, I wasn't convicted but I was investigated.' What would that have done in my life just so that somebody could score a political point?

KATE GRAHAM: After all of this, what do you make of our political climate for women as leaders?

ALISON REDFORD: I think it's expectations. If women are going to be in public life, they need to convey that they are perfect. And we fall into it. Maybe we accept this so people will accept us. I don't know. But we should be absolutely straightforward and not have it be a novelty or a curiosity. "Look. This is our family. We love each other and before I was ever in politics, I worked away from home. My daughter's father is a great father. He is as capable of taking care of Sarah as I am. And, yeah, sure, it's great when we're all together, but when we're not, we will survive. Maybe we don't all sit down and have dinner at the table every night, but I'm not sure many families do anymore. This is who we are." I shouldn't have had to pretend or keep this underlying message that we can keep it all together. We can keep the more traditional family structure together doing this because men can. Male politicians can. And there's this idea that if you were going to be a woman politician, you've still got to keep all the rest of it together. It's okay to say, "No, you can't, and you don't have to." Because that's not really what makes a family anyway. It doesn't do my family or anyone any good for me to not do what I want to do and live an unhappy life. What makes me happy is engaging in community, engaging with my family, being a better mother. And it doesn't have to conform to what my neighbour does. My neighbour doesn't expect me to conform to what she does, but we somehow have this underlying narrative that it's still got to be everything. It can't be everything. And that's okay.

KATE GRAHAM: What would you like to see change in Canadian politics so more women can lead and feel more able to be who they are?

ALISON REDFORD: We are a country of conservative institutions. Even though, as Canadians, we like to talk about being modern and diverse, we're not. Look at how we're represented and how elected officials are treated if they are in any way off of that norm—'that' being middle-aged white men. Somehow, we think Canadians are not like that, but we are. People fall into patterns really quickly and they aren't conducive to anyone out of the norm fitting into a political life....

It's going to take people like me, who have done it before, to say that what happened was wrong. I feel uncomfortable even saying all of this. Because I think there are women who we think of as Canadian feminist icons who will hear what I've said and really resist it. They won't like it. Nonetheless, I believe it's true based on my observations and that's all I can say. Not my experience, but my observation as to how this country works. I think it will take people who are prepared to break down those barriers. People liked me when I was nice. People liked me when I behaved the way they expected a female politician to behave. I hope that the next generation of women have a different experience....

When I look at my daughter, who she is and how she learned from my experiences, she's a very, very wise sixteen-year-old girl. And it's a shame she had to have that experience to learn. But my goodness, look out for her. I look at Sarah and her friends and they have a much stronger sense of who they are and how they define themselves. I hope that their understanding of the feminist dialectic and the women who they've seen come before them, that as they enter whatever career they choose, they have a wider variety of role models to identify with in terms of how people live their lives. I hope that's the case. Obviously, when you go through something, it changes who you are and how you think about yourself. I'm grateful that I went through that because I'm happy now with who I am and how I define myself. But I certainly define myself not just differently, but better than I did before. My daughter sometimes says, "You know, Mom, before you got involved in politics you went and did all this stuff in other places around the world. But"—and this is a sixteen-year-old talking—"we've got problems here. We've got problems with how minorities are treated, how women are treated, how we're dealing with gender identity. I mean, I live in a province where someone running for public office is talking about de-listing abortion so that it's no longer publicly funded." It's 2019.

We need people to engage and really talk about what it means to be a woman in Canada. Not a woman in politics, or a woman lawyer, or a woman anything-in-particular. Just a woman. And how we want to live our lives and how we should not have to conform. I didn't think when I left politics that there would be space to support women like this, I wasn't even sure that's what I wanted to do when I left politics. But it's important because we are still having the same ridiculous conversations. And we need to stop apologizing for having them. I hope we get to a place where the statistics are different and there's nothing exceptional about the fact that there will be as many women or more women in politics than men. That we have broken down the patriarchal system and that we don't even talk about it anymore. There is a complacency around patriarchy, and it is deeper than politics. It's the way women are portrayed in the media. It's the way we are portrayed in literature. It's the way we talk about female sexuality still. It is how we, as a society, work to contain the identity of women or try to contain the identity of women to a certain set of parameters. And we need to talk about it and to feel empowered to talk about it.

KATHLEEN WYNNE

PREMIER OF ONTARIO
(2013-2018)

"Sorry, not sorry."

This was the message former Ontario premier Kathleen Wynne sent to millions of voters in the final throes of the 2018 Ontario election. It was an acknowledgement of the political dynamics at play: Wynne was unpopular, and this had become the overarching narrative in the election.

In her famed final ad, Wynne looks disarmingly into the camera. "I'm sorry more people don't like me," she says, "but I'm not sorry for keeping business taxes low…or covering tuition for hundreds of thousands of students." She was also not sorry for a host of other policy initiatives, such as raising minimum wage and introducing rent control during her time as premier and leader of the Ontario Liberal Party.

If ever there was an ad that reflected one of the central challenges for female leaders, this was it.

Kathleen Wynne was born in Toronto in 1953. Her father was a doctor, and her mother was a musician. She attended public schools in Toronto before earning degrees at Queen's University, the University of Toronto, and the Ontario Institute for Studies in Education. She co-founded Citizens for Local Democracy in opposition to the amalgamation of Metro Toronto as well as the Toronto Parent Network to improve public education.

Wynne first ran for office in 1994, for the position of Toronto school trustee. She lost by seventy-two votes. She remained active in local advocacy work and ran again in 2000. During the campaign, her opponents labelled Wynne as an "extremist lesbian."

She ran again, beginning what would become a remarkable political rise. In 2003, Wynne won a nomination race in Don Valley West, defeating an incumbent cabinet minister to become an MPP [member of provincial parliament]; in 2004, she was appointed parliamentary assistant to the minister of education, and in 2006, she held the post. She led several ministries and ran for leader of the Ontario Liberal Party in 2013. Wynne won, becoming Ontario's first—and to date, only—female premier. She led the Ontario Liberal Party through her first general election in 2014, winning an unexpected majority mandate. In 2018, Wynne sought re-election and lost; her party's presence in the legislature was reduced from fifty-five seats to just seven.

Unlike the other interviews conducted for this project, this conversation was not my first time meeting Kathleen Wynne. I was already, decidedly, a fan. We met in 2017 when I was considering running as a candidate for the Ontario Liberal Party. I knew her policy record. I had a sense of what she was all about. What I was struck by in that first interaction was her obviously bright mind, high energy, and warm demeanour. I saw Kathleen on numerous occasions during the 2018 campaign, including speaking at rallies and during conversations among the team of candidates. I watched the grace with which she led, even as the campaign unravelled around her.

This time, we met in her home, and she made me a cup of tea and spoke with that same brightness, clarity, and warmth I recalled from our first meeting. The honesty and vulnerability with which she described her political highs and lows made me catch my breath. This was a woman I'd quit a job to run for and then had lost an election, at least in part, because of—yet throughout our interview two words often ran through my mind:

Not sorry.

"Pushing against the status quo was what needed to happen."
Kathleen Wynne was sorry people didn't like her as premier
of Ontario but not sorry for the policy advances she achieved.

KATHLEEN WYNNE: I'm the eldest of four girls—my parents had three of us in three years. It was a very intense childhood; that's how I think of it. I grew up being the organizer of two and then three kids. There's a picture of me walking along a country road and I've got my two sisters' hands. I'm about five, and they are four and three. I've got them by the arms and they're trying to pull back and I'm pulling them ahead. And when I look at it, it's sort of the image of my life. I'm in charge of these two kids. I'm taking them somewhere and they don't necessarily want to go. I would come home from school when I was in Grade 1, and I thought the best thing in the world was to play school. I was a teacher. They were so not interested in being the students. Those are some of my earliest memories....

As I grew up, we were not a partisan political household, but everyone was always interested in politics. I grew up in Richmond Hill, born in 1953, and so Richmond Hill was a small town north of Toronto. My dad was a general practitioner. My grandfather had been a general practitioner as well, in north Toronto, and he was alive until I was nine, so I had my grandparents. My mom—I would basically describe her as a shit disturber. If there was a council or a board of education to be challenged about some injustice, she was there. She was a member of the Social Planning Council at one point and was the catalyst behind a youth drop-in centre for kids who were kind of lost in the 1960s. I grew up in a household where, if there were problems to be solved, we had a responsibility to be part of solving them. We weren't bystanders, even though we weren't part of the elected official political world. My grandmother was born in 1888 and didn't have the vote until she was in her thirties, so there was no way you would ever miss an election. She voted in every single election and impressed upon us how important it was to vote. Our kitchen table was like an early Monty Python skit. Anytime you wanted to join in an argument, you just had to walk into our dining room. Whether it was music or something that was happening with the local council or the War Measures Act. It just depended on the year. Bob Dylan, Martin Luther King Junior, Pierre Elliott Trudeau; they were the people my family looked up to and held as models because they were all pushing against the status quo. And as far as my family was concerned, pushing against the status quo was what needed to happen....

Going out into the world, I was prepared to look for places where decisions were being made. I was probably on the confrontational side in terms of whether decisions were good or not. In high school I got involved in governance issues around the school board and the rules in our school. I mean, I tell the story all the time about girls not being able to wear pants to school. So, we had a little protest when I was in Grade 9 or 10 and a bunch of us came to school wearing pants; we were sent home again, even when we brought notes from our mothers. We were sent home again and again, until we finally got the rule changed. I mean that's a tiny example, but it led to when I was in Grade 11 or 12 bringing what we called Women's Libbers from downtown Toronto to come up and talk about women's rights. And we took a lot of flak from the boys in the school, but also from some girls. It helped me understand that I couldn't assume who was going to be onside and who wasn't.

KATE GRAHAM: The election that is often cited as your first race was the 1994 school board race, but you also ran for student council when you were a kid.

KATHLEEN WYNNE: Yeah, I did. But I didn't run for president. I was acclaimed as secretary. It's funny…I look back on it and think, 'Why didn't I run for president?' And I stepped aside for my male classmates. There's no doubt about it. I started high school in 1966 and, although we were in the midst of the turmoil of the sixties, it was not in this suburban town I was growing up in. It was not acceptable to be vocal about the position of women. In my household, in my small circle of friends, there was a lot of agitation and indignation about the way women were treated. I think from a very early age, having grown up in an all-girl family and just assuming that I could do whatever was presented, I think it was a rude awakening to get into school and realize that I wasn't going to be able to play with the big blocks because they were for the boys, and I was supposed to be in the doll centre. In 1958, when I started school, there was much more delineation in that way. I always rebelled against that. I always felt like that wasn't fair. I think I can safely say that as I went through school, I did have a bit of a chip on my shoulder about where we were put as women, and I think that was part of the motivation for me all through my life—to correct that—because it just felt wrong....

I remember my grandmother talking about how she had to stop teaching when she got pregnant. It was 1924, and my grandfather had come home from the first war. He'd been wounded over in Europe for a while. When he came back, she ran his office. But she loved teaching. She loved that independence, and she loved that sense of self. And I always felt she lost that a bit. With my mother, who was a singer and a performer, she made the decision to stop when she had all these babies, and she never went back to it. She became a play therapist and had a full career from the time I was a teenager. But I always felt that she was robbed of those years when she would have been building her show business career. I mean, she's ninety now. I know that she looks back on that time as her real self and wishes she had been able to do that.

There was some sadness around women's opportunities that I grew up with and that I think fuelled my sense of indignation. But when I was in high school, I wasn't there yet. I was unable to say, 'Why wouldn't I run for president? That's where I want to be. I want to be leading this team.' But I didn't. And then there was a hiatus. I didn't really get involved in university politics. I went to Queen's and then the University of Toronto for a master's degree. I don't really know the reason, but I think there were other things going on in my life. I was sorting out other relationship issues. I didn't really spend a lot of time involved in politics in university.

KATE GRAHAM: With those influences of your grandmother and mother, and this sadness about the loss of opportunity when family pressures came along, did you know that you would want both a successful career and to have a family?

KATHLEEN WYNNE: I made assumptions about what I would do. I assumed that I would have children. I don't know that I ever questioned that. And that's probably to the detriment of my conscious decision-making. I wanted to have kids, although I didn't sit around dreaming about having kids. That wasn't my raison d'être.

I assumed I would always have a career and that I would always be involved in the working world outside the home. I did a master's degree in adult education when my kids were very little. I remember debating with some younger women about who was a "real feminist" and what you had to do to really live to your full potential. One track we got off on was that women had to leave the home and take on roles men traditionally had. I just don't think that's the way we're all going to be the healthiest. I think we're going to be at our healthiest when people can do the things they want and that they're suited for—and gender doesn't provide a barrier to that. Because right now gender and poverty and other factors stand in the way of people doing the things they're best suited to. So yes, I wanted to have a full career, but if I'm going to have these three kids, I need to be able to do something that's going to allow me to look after these kids as well. I recognize that I have the privilege of being middle-class to be able to think in that way. So, from the time my kids were little, I was always working part-time, and politics entered into the realm of possibility when the kids started school. I was involved in their schools and board committees. That was the most important to me. That's why I ran for school board. I never had any interest in running for city council. It was education that drove me. That's why I ran for office in 1994.

KATE GRAHAM: In the years leading up to that, you were quite involved in "small-p politics." Could you speak a little bit to some of your other activism as an adult?

KATHLEEN WYNNE: It changed in the 1990s. My first child was born in 1980, and we lived in the Netherlands. I arrived back here in 1981, having finished my Master's in Linguistics and having to decide about whether I was going to be able to do a PhD or whether I was going to take another path. I came back and started teaching at Humber College. I taught language skills and determined I wasn't going to do a PhD. At that point, I got involved in local community issues, working at the school as a volunteer. One of the first things I did as a parent activist was walking a picket line with teachers when we were advocating for more arts education. I had my son—who was in Grade 2 at the time—by the hand and another one in a snuggly on my front. I was being trained in community organizing. Then in 1995, when Mike Harris was elected, it all changed. It ramped up the need for people to be involved. I found myself opposing the amalgamation of the City of Toronto, opposing the amalgamation of the school boards in the GTA, opposing the cutback of the social assistance rates, the 21 per cent social assistance rate cutback Harris invoked. I felt so strongly that he was breaking the social contract I'd grown up with, that we could continue to progress as an inclusive society; that our government would work to make the playing field more level; that we didn't have to accept that they were going to be "haves" and "have nots" but instead that people could continue to improve their lot in life. And what he basically said was, "No. There are going to be some people who are going to be okay and others who are not going to be okay. There are going to be kids who are going to fall through the cracks because we're not going to put the supports in place that are needed in school." I fundamentally disagreed. He said, "At the same time, we're going to impose our will on municipalities. We are not going to listen to what municipalities are saying. We're not going to listen to the experts." I was fundamentally opposed to that lack of evidence and lack of rational thinking around public policy....

I started a group with a few other women. We were sitting around the kitchen table at my house trying to decide what we were going to do. I think it was two hundred bucks that [Harris] sent everybody—you know, as a result of the cuts that he was making to government services, everybody got a two-hundred-dollar cheque. And we were just livid because I'm sure there were a lot of people for whom two hundred dollars was a really big deal. We didn't need the two hundred dollars and we knew perfectly well that our two hundred dollars would have been better spent on people who needed it in services. So, we were trying to figure out, "How do we pool this? How do we reach out and gather people together to do something about this?" And at the same time, John Sewell, a former mayor of Toronto, was organizing in the city. John Sewell and Gerard Kennedy had started this thing called the Together Group and they were pulling together people with basically the same concerns that we had. A friend of mine said to me, "You should phone John Sewell." I was like, "I am this young mom in north Toronto.

He is not going to want to talk to me!" I was wrong. I called him and he was very interested in what we were doing in north Toronto. He came up and he sat in one of our meetings and listened to what I was doing. Then he invited me to come and meet with his group, and out of that came Citizens for Local Democracy. Shortly after Harris cut social services and sent the two-hundred-dollar cheques, he moved into the amalgamation of the cities and that really blew up the activist community in Toronto. And in other parts of the province as well. So, we started meetings. We had these Monday night meetings and John Sewell was kind of my mentor. After about three or four meetings…he's an impulsive guy and he gets impatient with people, and I'm pretty good at running a meeting. I said to him one night, "John, would you like me to try running these?" He said, "Oh, that'd be great…."

I started running the meetings. For two years, every Monday night, whether it was at the Metropolitan United Church or whether it was the one we had on the referendum on the amalgamation in Massey Hall. Two years of Monday night meetings and we'd have up to two thousand people—at our peak. It was huge. It was this massive movement. And we failed—but we activated a lot of people in the policies that Harris was bringing in. There were people coming from all over the GTA and way beyond as well. Ted McMeekin, the mayor of Flamborough at the time, would pull people in to be speakers. So that gave me the most unbelievable two-year course in community organizing. I think it was during that period that I really learned that people were just people, whether they had a famous name or not, that they were open to being part of something important and meaningful….

At the same time, I started the Metro Parent Network, a subset of people who were more concerned about the amalgamation of the school boards. We were very worried about the education cuts. That's when People for Education started. In that time there were a lot of us, particularly a group of women, who got very involved in the activist community who then went on to elected office.

KATE GRAHAM: Let's talk about running for elected office. Tell me about taking the leap to run for the school board.

KATHLEEN WYNNE: My eldest was in high school. I was concerned enough about some of the things happening at the board, and I wanted to be involved. I guess one of the biggest issues for me was, "How do we do this?" Jane and I didn't know what this meant. I felt I had something to offer to the education discussion, but we didn't know how to get there. I didn't have any experience in party politics. I didn't have any connections to people who had run campaigns. It was pretty funny. We tried to find someone to run our campaign, and we talked to one Liberal operative, and he said, "Is she a Liberal?" He was talking to Jane. He said, "Because I'll work for a Labrador if she's a Liberal." Jane had to say, "Well, she's not a card-carrying anything. But she's a good person." We couldn't get him. Nobody wanted to work with us.

KATE GRAHAM: I'm sure that person is kicking themself now. [laughs]

KATHLEEN WYNNE: So, we did it ourselves. We got maps. Jane's a really good list person. Both her parents were engineers. She can take apart a problem and figure out what the component parts are, and she doesn't get overwhelmed. I want to go out and save the world, and she's got the list and telling me who I need to talk to in order to save the world. That's kind of how our relationship has gone. We got the maps; we combed our lists of class parents and our friends. We looked at our church membership list and called the people who were our friends. We had a little launch in our backyard in north Toronto. We were going to need money. We were going to need people to knock on doors and we were going to need people to help us put literature together. We basically found those people in our immediate circle and launched our campaign. And we decided, well, here's the map and here are all the houses. If I can get to knock on all these houses, then I've got a good chance at being elected.

We only lost by seventy-two votes. It was a great campaign and there are still people on my broad support team who worked with us in 1994. That little campaign was a bonding experience. But losing by only seventy-two votes—it was painful. I mean, the day after I was just in a sobbing mass on the floor because we worked so hard. But that only lasted a day and we'd come so close. We ran against a really strong incumbent trustee, so the odds were stacked against me. But we got so close, and I loved the exercise. I loved the permission that was granted by running for office. The permission to go up to a stranger's door, knock, and have a real conversation about their kids' lives, about education, about what they believe, about the kind of society we want to live in. I just loved it. And to this day if I'm feeling down or tired, if I go and knock on a few doors, I feel better about the world. Because people are wonderful people. They always have a story to tell about what's going on in their lives and that is what politics is for me.

KATE GRAHAM: So, the next time around....

KATHLEEN WYNNE: Toward the end of the 1990s, I thought I would try to run for the province because I believed in what Dalton McGuinty was doing; by that time, I was running under the Liberal banner. I ran for nomination in St. Paul's. That was a full-blown campaign. Michael Bryant was the favoured son at that point, he'd been at it a lot longer, and he won. But again, I learned a lot about the party; how the party mechanics worked, how I was going to manage that partisan piece, because I really hadn't experienced that.

I needed to get to know the people writing policy and figure out where my allies were, and decide whether I would try again. I lost the election in 1994. I lost the nomination in 1999. I worked in the provincial election in Don Valley West and decided I'd just do a little side work there because I lived on the border of Eglinton, Lawrence, St. Paul's, and Don Valley West. There were some people who were saying, "Well, why didn't you go and contest the nomination in Don Valley West?" And I thought about doing that. But when I found out that Paul Davidson had been working so hard and so long and he was about to get the nomination, I realized I didn't want to enter a race like that. I really didn't want to sour the relationship because that's what would have happened. He was a great candidate. He was a lovely man. I would've had to be very disruptive in that process. It wasn't the riding I lived in, and it wasn't a riding I had done a lot of work in. And it would have been simply to have a place to run for the nomination. That decision turned out to be absolutely critical in my political career because Andrew Bevin was the campaign manager for Paul Davidson. He was John Godfrey's principal secretary. And because Jane and I both worked hard in that Don Valley West election and didn't disrupt that process, Andrew and I got to know each other. We became really close, and he ran my subsequent campaigns. So, in 2003, when Paul determined he wasn't going to run again, Andrew knew me well enough and offered to run my campaign. That was a turning point. In the interim period, I had run for school trustee and won. I was on the school board when I ran provincially. So that was an important decision, and it was part of learning about being a team player.

KATE GRAHAM: So, how did you find doing politics within a partisan system?

KATHLEEN WYNNE: We had a pretty open caucus. Dalton McGuinty allowed for lots of commentary, and I always felt that I was heard. I always felt there was a place. But I felt the loss of some of my NDP and [Progressive] Conservative friends. On the school board, we ran the political spectrum, and I missed that range of opinions. But I also felt that in the Liberal caucus there was enough room that I could be comfortable, which is why I chose the Liberal Party. I believe that that centre big tent is really where I'm most comfortable.

KATE GRAHAM: Let's talk about the time from when you were an MPP up to the period where you start running for leader. You held many significant cabinet portfolios during that time.

KATHLEEN WYNNE: I held a number of portfolios, but the three years when I was not a minister were very important. I feel lucky that I had the opportunity to serve on committees and be a backbencher, to get to know how the system worked before I was thrown into a ministerial position. Once you're a minister, you have less opportunity to see what's happening across government. As a backbencher serving on cabinet committees, you see everything. Everything comes your way, and you get to speak on everything in the House. You get a broad education about what is happening in government. it was very clear to me that the legislature was an old boys' club. It was very male-dominated. It was starting to change, but the institution was male and so was our party structure. When we first formed government, for example, we didn't have a policy on poverty reduction. We formed a women's caucus, led by Deb Matthews, who made the case to our caucus that we should have a policy position on and a strategy for poverty reduction. There was some discussion about who our voters were. And I remember standing up and saying, "Well, yeah, okay, people who are living in deep poverty may not vote for us. But there are lots of people who do vote for us who care about that, and that shouldn't be the reason we would do it." So that's not sexism per se, except that it was an issue that had not been raised by the men and it reinforces the research that when you have a critical mass of women at the table, different issues get discussed. Different perspectives are brought forward.

KATE GRAHAM: Tell me a bit about your time as minister of education. You got into politics because of education. When that portfolio came along, were you thinking, "This is the peak of my political career," or was this a departure point for something more?

KATHLEEN WYNNE: I was so, so excited...so excited....

KATE GRAHAM: [laughs]

KATHLEEN WYNNE: In 2006, Sandra Pupatello was the minister of education. She'd only been there for about five months and, I'll be honest, I had been disappointed that I hadn't had the opportunity to be considered for a ministerial role up until that point. But I think everybody has those feelings. I was in Cobourg or somewhere in Eastern Ontario, trying to get a meeting with the premier to talk about a policy we were looking at that would remove kids' driver's licenses if they dropped out of school. I was deadly opposed. I thought it was a crazy idea and I was really worried about it. And so, it was the night before the caucus retreat, and I got a call. I was really excited. I really, honestly did not think that this was me being offered a ministerial post. When I went in, and he sat me down and said, "You want to be the minister of education?" It was almost that abrupt, like, "Oh, my God. I don't even know what to say."

I was just flabbergasted. It was a big surprise. I remember that I was so flustered that as we were leaving, I said, "Premier, can I fix the driver's license thing?" And he was like, "Oh, for heaven's sake. Yes."

I was very excited and it did feel a bit like a dream. I remember my first briefings. I had to really hold myself back because I was interested in everything. Every time I had a briefing, I wanted to dive into the issue whether it was facilities condition or the transportation file, the school bus file, or curriculum, I was just so interested in how it all fit together. And I was excited about the opportunity to talk with these great people so we could really move. It was a real dream. But I didn't think of it as the pinnacle of my career. That's not how I framed it in my mind. When I was shuffled out three-and-a-half years later, in 2010, I was devastated. I loved it so much.

KATE GRAHAM: Let's roll the clock forward a little bit and talk about leadership. The party has already been in power for about ten years. The premier says he's going to step down. Tell me what that thought process looked like.

KATHLEEN WYNNE: I had been the minister of education, the minister of transportation, and municipal affairs. I was in the ministry of what was called at that time Aboriginal affairs. I was the minister of those two ministries when Dalton stepped down. He had done me a great service allowing me to serve in all of those ministries. Even though I was devastated when I was taken out of education and put in transportation, it was the best thing that ever happened in my political career because I got a much broader view of government. By the time the premier stepped down in 2012, I felt it was something I should consider. People had been talking to me a bit before that, about whether I would run if he stepped down. There was speculation about when. So, I'd been thinking about it. And when he called us into the caucus room that night at six o'clock in the evening for this bizarre caucus meeting—we didn't know what was going to happen. And the minute he said that he was stepping down, I knew I had to think very seriously about getting the people around me who were going to help me make the decision. And I did. I did not expect to win. I was not the odds-on favourite to win the leadership by a long shot....

Jane and I had a conversation. First of all, she was going through breast cancer. We had sold our house. We were renovating a smaller house we were going to move into. And she was deciding whether she had to have chemotherapy or not. Turns out she didn't. But I had made a personal decision that if she had to go through chemo, I wouldn't run for the leadership. It just would have been too hard on the family. She had radiation and, having that knowledge under our belt, we decided that we would go for it. Because these are family decisions, they're not individual decisions. I had to know that she was going to be okay with another level of profile, even if I didn't win. She asked me, "How are you going to feel if you're not part of the debate?" That was the deciding question for me. I knew that I would feel disappointed in myself if I didn't at least try to be part of the discussion.

KATE GRAHAM: You went into it not feeling that you would likely emerge as the winner, but you did win. Tell me about that moment, becoming the first female premier in Ontario.

KATHLEEN WYNNE: It was thrilling. It was so thrilling. I loved my leadership speech. I had written it largely myself. Obviously, we worked it over and over and over again, and other people had input. But I had sat at the kitchen counter and written it, and I loved that I didn't have the expectation that I was going to win. I could say exactly what I needed to say. I wanted to be very clear with people that I was a lesbian, that it was something they had to think long and hard about because that was going to be a big deal. Not only was I a woman but I was from the LGBTQ community and that was going to be a big deal for the people of the province. But in my speech I said that I believed in the people of Ontario and that it was not going to be an issue. And I believed in the party members and that it was not going to be an issue. But there had been people who'd come to me and said, "You shouldn't run because you can't win. You can't be the premier because you're a lesbian. You won't get elected." Quite apart from what they may have felt about me personally, they felt I couldn't win. I said to them, "That's how homophobia works. It works by keeping people out of positions, not by including every-one in the race." So, I put that into my leadership speech, and I just felt totally exhilarated when the numbers came in that we'd done it. It was quite a moment.

KATE GRAHAM: So now you're the premier. Tell me a bit about the early experience of being a premier.

KATHLEEN WYNNE: I was the first female premier, but I'd never been a male premier. I'd never been premier. And so, it was just all new. We were in a minority parliament. We had a lot of baggage. The issue around gas plants, that was very contentious. I spent a lot of time in that first year trying to find a way to open up the processes, open up the information, let people know what had gone on so that, by the time an election came, we'd be able to put some of that behind us. I apologized for things that had happened because I'd been part of the government. I spent a lot of time in that first year doing that. I don't know the extent to which my being a woman allowed me to do some of those things in a way that maybe a man wouldn't have. I think maybe that's the case. I'm not sure. But I certainly knew that I wanted to confront those things....

It was more people being excited and coming up to me, bringing their daughters to me and saying, "I want my daughter to know she can do anything she wants to." The fact that there were six female premiers in that first year.... I had the privilege of chairing the Council of the Federation in Niagara-on-the-Lake. It just happened that Ontario was in the rotation. And so, I got to chair the premiers' table when there were six women at the table, which was almost half. It was an exhilarating time and it felt like we were breaking ground. Having Deb Matthews, my good friend, as the deputy premier, and having Liz Sandals as the minister of education—we joked about the grandmothers running the place. It was really empowering to a lot of women to see us in those offices, and putting into the budget things that were going to directly impact women's lives, like increasing funding for early childhood educators and childcare workers. I had male colleagues say to me, "These things wouldn't be happening if there wasn't a woman in that chair." I was proud we were able to do those things. And if it was because I was a woman, then that's okay.

KATE GRAHAM: In the beginning, then, there was all kinds of excitement and enthusiasm, and that carried into the 2014 election....

KATHLEEN WYNNE: Yeah. There was certainly no expectation that we would win the 2014 election.

KATE GRAHAM: And you won a majority! And then things started to turn. When you think back, what was the earliest moment where you knew that things were going to start turning in a different direction?

KATHLEEN WYNNE: It was about two years into our 2014 mandate and about three years into being premier. The numbers were changing. We weren't doing as well in people's eyes as we had been, and my personal numbers were going down. I think it was indicative of the high expectations we had for ourselves, but also the high expectations people had for us. We had a lot of support in Ontario well into those first two years. I was popular. The *Toronto Star* sometimes callled me "the popular premier." And then that started to change. The issues [allegations of corruption] around the Sudbury by-election got very political. It became a real political hot potato. In the end, there was no wrongdoing. However, it was a hit to us as a party and to my brand in terms of, "We thought she was something different, and then here she is involved in the political machinations." I mean, I was the leader of the party. I was going to have to be involved in all sorts of things. But I think people they didn't want to see me involved in those things, they wanted me to be different somehow. But it was never clearly articulated what different meant. In the opinion research, people had started to feel like, "Oh, well, she's just like the others."

And then the partial sell-off of Hydro One. The fact was, I'd made a commitment to build transit. We needed cash because we couldn't just borrow all the money, so we needed to raise some of that cash and we did a year-long process to determine how. We decided to broaden the ownership of Hydro One. That was the most challenging political issue we had to deal with. That wasn't what kept me up at night. I worked very hard to make sure that anything we did around Hydro One wasn't going to hurt people.

It wasn't going to raise electricity prices. And it wasn't going to affect their delivery of power. It could actually improve their delivery of power. But it was the hardest political issue because it became about whether I believed in privatization or public power. And whether I was being true to myself in supporting the public good. That was what the NDP chose to make of it. It became a very difficult political issue. It was the go-to for both the third party and the opposition at every turn.

KATE GRAHAM: I recall it became very personal. It was about you. "Unplug Wynne" signs started showing up. This may be an unfair question, but if you had been a man in the role, do you think there would have been that same opportunity to make this so much about you personally?

KATHLEEN WYNNE: It's an interesting question because there were lots of ads run about Dalton as well. So, I think there would have been an attempt to do the same thing, but I'm not sure it would have taken the same nasty turn. The depth of my unlikability was pretty severe, and I'm just not sure whether that was all about our policies or whether there was an element of "We're sick of her because she's a woman. She's a lesbian and I put up with it. I held my nose and voted, or I stayed at home the first time but I'm not going to do it again because she really bugs me." I think there was an element of that. And then the vile things that got said on social media became part of the narrative and I'm not sure that would have happened to the same degree....

Trump being elected in 2016 [became] really vile permission for misogyny that reached across the border and became part of the narrative here as well. I think it was a confluence of things. But I do think that the fact that we'd been in office for fifteen years can't be discounted. I think it was part of what happened in the election in 2018, but it's not everything. There were other things going on.

KATE GRAHAM: Let's talk about the 2018 election. What was that election like for you?

KATHLEEN WYNNE: It was a hard, hard campaign—like it was almost a foregone conclusion that we were going to lose. And that was really hard. I had to continue to believe it was possible to win because we had fantastic candidates all over the province. They were running great campaigns and were hearing at the door that people liked the stuff we were doing. But I knew that they were also hearing that people didn't like me. It was a tough campaign because I felt like I was the problem and I felt so responsible for what was happening....

We made that decision the week before the election to say to the people of the province that I knew I wasn't going to be the premier. That was a really hard day in my political life. The numbers were not moving. We were very worried about winning any seats at all. I just couldn't believe that we were that far down. It was devastating. I also knew that as soon as I stood up and said, "I'm not going to be the premier," that there would be candidates all over the province who would feel so upset and so deflated and their teams would be deflated. But I also knew there were candidates who needed that, who would be able to go out and say, "Okay, she's not going to be the premier. You can vote for me without worrying about whether she's going to be in the premier's seat." So that was a really painful juncture. It was very, very hard. I felt that I had let people down. And that was never what I wanted to do. That was the last thing I wanted. I always felt that I wanted to lead from the middle, from the heart of the team, and to feel that I was the thing getting in the way of good people getting elected, it was just the most painful thing....

After the election, I was devastated. I felt like there was a real burden that I hadn't carried the way I needed to. I was humiliated. I was sad for all the great candidates who had lost, and I felt deeply responsible for what had happened. Part of that was related to my experience in 2014, when we had won and there had been a lot of talk about how my presence as the leader had helped us win. It was like the mirror reflection of that. If I'd been such a help in 2014, clearly 2018 was the opposite. I would say I'm still not over that completely. I still feel responsible. I know intellectually that there were lots of things going on. It's just that I felt personally connected to people in the party and I feel that I should have figured it out. There was a conversation about whether I should step down a year and a half or so before the election, and I really thought long and hard about that. I talked to people. I listened to the opinion research and determined that there wasn't anybody better positioned to win, but there probably wasn't anybody in a better position to lose either. That was a really tough decision. The fact is, I was in my first mandate. I had won an election in 2014. I'd made a commitment to a plan that we were implementing, and I felt strongly that I wanted to see that through. And to throw the party into a leadership race a year and a half out from an election when I'd only been there since 2013 did not seem like a recipe for success. So, I put my money on us being able to carry it through and it didn't work.

KATE GRAHAM: Do you think the expectations on you were realistic?

KATHLEEN WYNNE: The expectations of women are very mixed up. It feels like you've got to be all these things. You've got to be mother, grandmother, strong economic politician, strong on social issues and social justice. You've got to do all this stuff. If you do it all too well, then you're getting above yourself or, like, "Who does she think she is?" There's an element of, "She thinks she's so smart and we don't like that. We don't want her talking down to us." It was very hard for me to figure out exactly the tone and the presentation. We would have these ridiculous conversations about scarves and colours that I should or should not wear. I've got cupboards of scarves upstairs. Toward the end of my time as premier there was, "Well you shouldn't wear so many scarves because people think that looks like you're rich." Some of those scarves cost ten dollars. There was confusion about 'who we want her to be' that seeped into the narrative. The less popular I was, the more panicked people were about, "Are you wearing the right makeup? Are you wearing the right clothes? Are you showing up just right?"

KATE GRAHAM: So few women have served in our most senior political roles and their tenure tends to be less than that of men. What do you think that says about us as Canadians?

KATHLEEN WYNNE: There's the "she wears on me" thing. We are just not used to having women in leadership roles. I think it's going to take some time and it's going to take more female leaders to get us there. The expectations of women are higher in some ways but less clearly articulated. If you have really high expectations, it's easier for that person to fall off the pedestal. We don't really have a handle on what those expectations of women are. You want someone who is a nurturing mother figure? Or is it that you want someone who's a hard ass and can get things done? Or do you want a woman to be everything? I think that's actually the answer: We're meant to be everything. We're meant to be tough, smart, and nurturing, and loving, and emotional and all of those things all at the same time. And the fact is that we can be those things, some of the time. But to be all of them all of the time is impossible. I think that gets us into trouble as a country in terms of keeping a woman in leadership for a longer period of time.

KATE GRAHAM: And you had the added dimension of homophobia.

KATHLEEN WYNNE: Yeah. We absolutely experienced homophobia. And it was explicit in some cases. There was always homophobic literature distributed throughout my political career in election campaigns. There were many people who came to me when I was running for the leadership to say, "Don't. I don't think you can win." And then when I was premier, Jane wouldn't always come to everything. There were places I went that she didn't because it would have created a red flag. It would have been uncomfortable. We didn't make that decision often, but from time to time we decided we weren't going to go there—that was a pretty profound example of how I had to adjust my life to the realities of a homophobic society.

KATE GRAHAM: I'm sure you've had a lot of these conversations with other women who are thinking about running, and many decide not to. What do you hear as the most common reasons?

KATHLEEN WYNNE: There's an adage that you have to ask a woman three times and you just have to show the man the application form. Women will say to me, "I don't have enough experience. I don't know if I could do it. I don't know how I would balance family. I don't know how I would raise the money." Those are the barriers that women throw up—but I think that the fundamental one is that many, many, many women just don't feel that they are able to do it. And I think that's partly because they haven't seen a lot of women in these roles. They don't see themselves reflected and what you have to do to get there all seems a bit mysterious.

KATE GRAHAM: You've experienced all the highs and lows that politics has to offer, so when others come looking to you for advice—knowing how difficult it can be but also how important it is—what do you say to them?

KATHLEEN WYNNE: Think about what you care about. Follow those paths. Find the people who are like-minded to be on your team. You need a core team. Those are the people who are going to be your touchstone. You'll get lots of advice from lots of people. There will be lots of negativity. You will need a group of people you can trust. You need to have people who are around you for all the right reasons. Because they know you care about education or you care about healthcare, or you've had an experience in your life or in your family that has motivated you to get involved in politics, and that's what you can't lose sight of....

The other thing is it's totally worth it. It's tough, but it is totally worth having the opportunity to influence people's lives for the better. I have always felt that it's a privilege to have had enough support in my life that I was able to do this. I've always believed that because of the privileges I've had, it's my responsibility to pay back to the community. And so, if you are interested in politics and you have the ability and support to do it, it is totally worth it because you will make a difference. Even if you run a campaign and you don't win, you still will have touched hundreds and hundreds of lives. You'll knock on a door and some little girl will come to the door, and she'll see a female politician on the doorstep, and she'll know that's possible. It's worth it from day one.

SECOND CHANCES

On April 16, 2019, Rachel Notley lost her bid for re-election as Alberta's seventeenth premier. Two months later, she took the stage at the Canada 2020 *No Second Chances* event in Ottawa to share reflections about the political environment for women.

> The nature of political debate is often very combative, so it attracts people who tend to be quite comfortable yelling at each other. Those with familial obligations will often balk at the long, unpredictable hours paired with the choice to spend so-called downtime building relationships with colleagues and stakeholders—and those who succeed in life by *delivering* results may be turned off by an environment where success is often measured by their ability to *talk* about delivering results. Those who pursue pragmatic problem-solving may be frustrated by the endless and exhausting positional conflict. In short, the opportunity is not equal. The rules of the game are not constructed to encourage participation where opportunity exists. Or to put another way, the rules of the game are not constructed by women.

Every election has its unique dynamics, and this was certainly true in Alberta in 2019. Longstanding but shifting partisan lines in the province were tested in 2015, and again in 2019. Notley was quick to urge the group not to chalk up the results of her recent loss to her gender but instead to economic and partisan forces. But, as she reminded the group, we also need to acknowledge that the playing field is far from even.

Imagine a race where half the runners enjoy the benefit of state-of-the-art, high-tech running shoes, and the other half have been given Crocs. Separate and apart from how ugly they are, we also know that the first group of runners would take off and do very well, while only a fraction of the runners in the Crocs would manage to keep up. Not only that, at the end of the race, the top finishers get to make the rules for the next race—so, lo and behold, the distribution of high-tech runners becomes limited and everyone else is told that in the next race, they'll be running in high heels. Not surprisingly, when the next race is complete, only one runner in high heels finishes in the top ten....

I would argue that up to now we have been preoccupied with the following strategies: First, we've celebrated that one high-heeled runner a lot. Second, we've asked that high-heeled runner to talk about how they learned to run so well in high heels. Third, we've spent a lot of time trying to encourage other people to join the sport of high-heeled running. And finally, we've even developed programs to provide special training to high-heeled runners. But you know what we haven't done yet? We haven't just *demanded* that everyone in the race be given their own freaking pair of running shoes.

Women are not equal—and I'm not just referring to politics. In fact, I would argue that the absence of women in politics is as much the symptom of the larger problem as it is the cause. It is both.

Experts in the field agree. Countries in which women do not enjoy equal rights and status tend to also see fewer women elected to political leadership roles; countries with few women in political leadership roles are less likely to advance policy solutions toward the empowerment and equal rights of women and girls. The same can be said about the underrepresentation of ethnic or racial groups, or any other "non-prototype" seeking participation in our political system.

In simpler terms: it's a self-reinforcing cycle that keeps some people in and some people out.

What does this cycle look like in practice? The interviews with the first ministers provide powerful and illustrative snapshots of obstacles to success for women. They too have experienced many of the well-documented barriers that women face at each stage of the political process: struggling with confidence and lack of knowledge or supports to navigate the system in making early decisions to run for office; challenges associated with taking on new roles in the first years holding political office; the too-often unfriendly or sexist environment on social media or in treatment of them by the press; the internal battles about how to present oneself and fend off imposter-syndrome tendencies. They also highlighted the added obstacles that seem unique to women serving in our most senior political roles.

First, female leaders are subject to irreconcilably conflicting expectations. Few Canadians understand the day-to-day realities of life as a political leader, regardless of gender. Political leaders live with unforgivingly hectic schedules that spread well into weekends and evenings. They are expected to be ready with informed comments on an enormous scope of topics and current events, maintain hundreds or thousands of relationships, and somehow have time to respond to every social media post and text message. Few people truly understand the strain that comes with the permanent loss of anonymity and relentless media scrutiny. Things that most people take for granted—like being able to take a break or a holiday—are much more difficult, and they are never fully away from the public eye. It is not unusual for people to make small missteps in their professional or personal lives, but only for political leaders do these moments become fodder for front pages and talk radio. The collective cost of these realities on personal well-being and family life can be enormous—for men and for women.

It is very normal in Canada for us to tire of our political leaders (and sometimes for them to tire of us!). Fresh election campaigns often promise change and progress in a way that makes it seem easy—if only those making the promises are delivered to office.

Once serving in government, however, the challenge of turning promises to new realities are much more difficult. Our leaders often fall short of what they promised and of what we expect, unrealistic as it may be. Thus, the political fortunes of most of our leaders include a distinct rise and fall. Few are afforded the luxury of going out on top, at the peak of their political careers. It's more common that public confidence and support will wane, followed by the leader's departure through a general election or otherwise.

The distinct difference for female leaders in Canada is that this decline comes much sooner. Female first ministers serve on average for about 60 per cent of men's tenure. Why is this?

As Christy Clark put it, it's the "dilemma that women face between being liked and being tough. You don't get to be both; men do. You can like a tough guy, but people don't like tough women—and people don't think women are tough enough if they like them. So, you're either one or the other or you're somewhere in between, and heaven forbid you're somewhere in between."

In Kathleen Wynne's words, "the depth of my unlikability was pretty severe and I'm just not sure whether that was all about our policies or whether there was an element of 'We're sick of her because she's a woman. She's a lesbian and I put up with it. I held my nose and voted, or I stayed at home the first time but I'm not going to do it again because she really bugs me.'" About women more generally she added, "We're meant to be everything. We're meant to be tough, smart, and nurturing, and loving, and emotional and all of those things all at the same time."

For Alison Redford, her political decline was marked with controversies including taking her young daughter on the plane with her while on official business. In her words, "There was still that idea that you're either the fairly traditional, typical female who juggles lots of things or you're the premier. If I ever went anywhere and took Sarah with me, we would make sure that our family paid for that ticket even though there already was a seat on the plane, and I may not have seen her for three weeks. If a man takes his child on the plane, he's a good dad."

This idea that you have to be everything is an impossible expectation that puts heightened pressure on women in senior roles of government, while also creating an environment in which it is more difficult for leaders to maintain public support. Our willingness to judge women as parents and partners—and in a way that is rarely a part of our evaluation or consideration of male leaders—is particularly problematic. The challenge of maintaining a reputation as "nice" or "likable" can also be at odds with making difficult or contentious decisions.

Political leadership is hard, no matter who is in the role, but layering on added points of evaluation for some but not all individuals in the role is akin to putting Crocs on the runners in a fixed race. We can critique their running ability all we like, but we have missed the point if we fail to acknowledge the unequal standards we have placed upon them. The product is a dynamic where female leaders are more likely to fall short of our expectations and lose our support as electors, thus reducing their average tenure in office and creating a steeper fall.

Second, there is evidence that female leaders are too often reduced to a transactional utility and their political demise can come early as a result. Because so few women have served in the top political roles, it is still something of a novelty in most parts of Canada. Only three subnational jurisdictions in Canada have had two female first ministers (Alberta, British Columbia, and the Northwest Territories); three have yet to have a female first minister (Saskatchewan, New Brunswick, and Nova Scotia). This novelty factor can be part of the reason why political parties and insider power brokers take interest in female leadership candidates in the first place: the promise of an electoral boost.

In Kim Campbell's words, "I think there is a certain Hail Mary pass that when you know you're in trouble, you try to find somebody who is the same only different to lead you. And the idea that by having Canada's first female prime minister you might get a leg up on what was going to be a very difficult political fight I think was attractive. But I also think that there may be some people who are less concerned that if you're a female then you fail. That sort of confirms some deep sense they have that maybe women aren't really cut out for this."

Several of the women's political demise came (or was expedited) within their own party. Kathy Dunderdale spoke about this dynamic:

In politics, we tend to be all A-type personalities. We all have strong ideas. You wouldn't run if you didn't have strong ideas about how the world ought to be. Most of us think we can make pretty good premiers. And so there tends to be, well, there can be a great collegiality if things are going well amongst a group of elected officials in a party, for example. There is also a great deal of competition. Because most people don't want to sit on the backbench. They wanted to be at the cabinet table. When things are good, things are usually pretty good. When things start to go sideways, and the polls are usually the first indicators of that, then things can get rough. And things can get rough in caucuses. And it doesn't take much…. When people start to think more about their own personal survival, a political party is not the venue where people are going to set all of that aside for the greater good. That's not how politics works, and I don't care what party you're in. It's what's politically expedient.

Female leaders face greater public expectations, which established a higher bar for maintaining public support. While they and their parties may benefit from the fanfare that comes with their novelty, this advantage erodes quickly. Political parties, hardwired to gain and hold political power, can turn on their female leaders as they lose public support by easily playing into existing narratives and perceptions. An official business trip with a young child in tow can too easily be spun into a spending scandal; a lesbian premier introducing changes to an education curriculum that includes a modernized curriculum about consent and gender is pushing "her agenda."

Fundamentally, as Rachel Notley said, "The rules of the game are not constructed by women."

How are we to remedy this? On June 19, 2019, the women who have served in our most senior political roles penned a letter to Canadians on what needs to change in our politics if we want to see more women lead.[7] We are wise to pay close attention to this guidance. Their recommendations include:

....

[7] The full text of the letter is contained on page 232.

1) *Raise the level of political discourse in Canada.*
   We must treat each other with civility, respect, and dignity, regardless of partisan or policy differences. We also need standards to enforce a civil decorum, including within legislatures, online, and in the media.

2) *Recruit more women and a greater diversity of women.*
   The letter calls on political parties specifically to make candidate recruitment a priority as well as fundamental changes to the processes to remove barriers faced by women.

3) *Close the gender gap in Canada.*
   This will require a concerted effort across jurisdictions, with a particular call for investments in childcare. Until we see more women and girls enjoying equal rights and status in Canada, we will not realize equitable political participation and women in leadership.

Each of the leaders featured in this book became engaged in politics for a specific reason. For Nellie Cournoyea, it was to ensure that there were people within the territorial government who understood the implications of the decisions being made. ("So when something came up, then there would be an explanation for it. Not a fight but an explanation.") Eva Aariak's political action started early, growing out of a deep connection to her community and sparking a remarkable political career that has produced substantive protections and language rights for Indigenous communities. Pat Duncan believed so strongly in the need for women's voices within her party that she ran while pregnant and took on the leadership of her party with young children at home. These women have different backgrounds but share a motivation to become engaged in politics so they could make specific changes to the world around them. The changes they wanted to make were informed by their own life experiences and passions.

Canada's "no second chances" problem is about more than the electoral fortunes of the few women who have served as a first minister, and it runs deeper than the underlying reasons often cited as to why we have not seen more women rise to our most senior political roles. It is about the cost of upholding systems of privilege within our politics.

When our political leadership roles are limited to those fitting a prototype shaped by systemic privilege—specifically of older, white, affluent, straight men—we limit the pool of people and talent we can draw upon to a small fraction of the population. We limit the experiences and motivations found in our most senior leaders to those with the life experiences and motivations of dominant groups, to the exclusion of others. We prevent underrepresented groups from breaking through and making the kinds of internal changes that may enable others to follow—that is, changing the rules of the game. We solidify unconscious biases—including in young children—about what it looks like to be a leader, and about who belongs and who does not, perpetuating the generational cost of shaping both how they view political leaders as well as their own aspirations or lack thereof. And, most importantly and problematically, we hinder our ability to make meaningful progress toward the broader project of addressing inequities in Canada.

This cost is too high.

No Second Chances is not a book about women not succeeding. It is about the implications when we as a nation do not succeed in addressing the power imbalances that have for too long produced inequities in our politics—and by extension, in our country.

Let us recognize the accomplishments of the thirteen women who have overcome these barriers to become first ministers. And let us resolve to work persistently, across and outside political parties, to eliminate the barriers that remain so it is no longer uncommon to see half a legislature filled with women, or half the complement of first ministers, or half of Cabinets.

Until we achieve the full and equal participation of all women—and a future in which second chances become not a historical first but a routine part of the political experience of all genders—there is more work to be done.

"For women and girls to aspire to be leaders, they need to see themselves in positions of power now…." (Left to right) Pat Duncan, Kathy Dunderdale, Catherine Callbeck, Kim Campbell, Alison Redford, Rachel Notley, and Kathleen Wynne at the *No Second Chances* Canada 2020 event in Ottawa, June 2019.

June 19, 2019

Dear Canadians:

Of the more than 300 first ministers in our country's history, only 12 have been women.

We are these women.

More than half of Canadians are women and girls, but women, in all their diversity, continue to be underrepresented in every level of politics. This is especially true in our most senior leadership roles. As of today, we have no female first ministers (prime ministers or premiers) in Canada.

We are a nation rich in diversity, talent, intellect and creativity. We are also a nation facing many pressing challenges. To meet these challenges, we need the very best from Canadians. All Canadians.

We must finish the work started more than a century ago when women pushed for their right to vote, to stand in elections, and to represent Canadians. We must be vigilant in protecting and extending what we have already accomplished. We must finally achieve the full and equal participation of women in all aspects of political life, from community activism to elected representation.

Over the past few months, we have shared our stories through Canada 2020's No Second Chances podcast, providing a perspective on some of the barriers women face in politics. Today, we come together to identify what needs to change if we want to see more women lead.

We need more women, and a greater diversity of women, in politics. This won't happen naturally. Political parties must make the recruitment and nomination of female candidates a priority. We call on all current First Ministers and all party leaders to put measures in place to recruit more women. This must go beyond setting targets; parties must make fundamental changes to these processes. We will never achieve parity in any legislature, or in positions of power, until we achieve gender parity among candidates. For women and girls to aspire to be leaders, they need to see themselves in positions of power now, and learn about the often forgotten history of women's leadership in our politics.

We must raise the level of political discourse in Canada. To have free and comprehensive debate, we must treat each other with civility, respect, and dignity, regardless of partisan or policy differences. We call on all members of all legislatures, the Speakers of our legislatures, House Leaders, and party leaders to insist on a higher standard of political discourse, making politics a place that is more welcoming to everyone. We call for this civility to be reflected in how news about politics is reported, analyzed, and discussed. Canadians — all of us — must hold ourselves to a higher standard in which misogyny, sexism, racism, hatred, and violence have no place in our politics.

Barriers that prevent women's political participation must be removed. We have made progress towards a fairer, more equitable society, but the work is not yet done. We must continue to push to close gender gaps in Canada. Investments in childcare are particularly important. We call on all jurisdictions to continue to take action to improve the status of women and girls, in all their diversity.

We have led different political parties and we do not agree on how to solve all of our policy problems. Diversity of opinion in our politics is a strength, not a weakness.

Emily Murphy once said, "Nothing ever happens by chance; everything is pushed from behind." To women who think they just aren't ready, we say to you that entering politics was one of the best things we ever did. Put your name on a ballot, and give it a go: you will create a future full of Second Chances.

Until we achieve the full and equal participation of women in politics, we will not reach our full potential as a nation. Generations of Canadians before us have pushed for the inclusion of women in politics, and it is time that we too rise to this challenge.

Sincerely,

Rita Johnston
Former Premier of
British Columbia

Nellie Cournoyea
Former Premier of the
Northwest Territories

Catherine Callbeck
Former Premier of
Prince Edward Island

Pat Duncan
Former Premier
of the Yukon

Eva Aariak
Former Premier
of Nunavut

Kathy Dunderdale
Former Premier of
Newfoundland & Labrador

Christy Clark
Former Premier of
British Columbia

Alison Redford
Former Premier
of Alberta

Kathleen Wynne
Former Premier
of Ontario

Rachel Notley
Former Premier
of Alberta

Kim Campbell
Former Prime
Minister of Canada

ACKNOWLEDGEMENTS

A few years ago, I reached out to Alison Loat to seek advice on a book idea about the political fortunes of female premiers in Canada. Alison, herself the author of a book about Canadian politics among other accomplishments, gave me some pointed advice: don't think about this like a book. Think about it like a project, find someone who will take it on with you, and a book can follow.

She was right.

The opportunity to closely examine Canada's female first ministers has turned out to be one of the great privileges of my life, sparking a successful podcast with Canada 2020, two spin-off books, and inspiring some of my own political adventures, including a leadership bid. I am indebted to the remarkable women who so willingly opened their homes and hearts to me, and whose words fill these pages. I have found myself reminded of things they said whenever I have encountered personal or political challenges, providing a great source of inspiration long after the interviews were complete. My hope is that their words yield similar value to others who read this book.

I owe an acknowledgement with gratitude to the team at Canada 2020 who believed in this project and made these interviews possible, including Anna Gainey, Alex Paterson, Mira Ahmad, Sarah Turnbull, and Carolyn Smith. The trip across Canada to conduct interviews was shared with Aaron Reynolds and Adam Caplan who played a special role in making it such a meaningful and thoughtful experience. The project was supported by Mastercard and made possible by Kate Karn, who continues to be the reason so many Canadians have had the chance to learn from our female leaders.

Turning a project into a book only happens with the support of a team. I am grateful for the extraordinary women at Second Story Press who believed in this project from the start, with special thanks to Margie Wolfe, Gillian Rodgerson, Bronte Germain, Melissa Kaita, and Andrea Knight. The Feminist History Society, and specifically Diana Majury, will also always have a special place in my heart for having played a critical role in the book's production, as the final project after a decade-long effort to preserve the stories of female leaders in Canada. Sarah Kabani from Huron University College also supported the book's completion, providing an excellent 'fact check' editorial review.

On a personal note, my text message chats with my mom, Susan Graham, and mother-in-law, Lee Helmer, were especially active during the writing of this book, full of helpful guidance on every decision from the title to the chapter framing to the final product. My husband, Jesse Helmer, continues to be my chief thought partner in this (and every) project, with a special skill for listening to (often half-baked!) ideas and expertly working alongside me to bring them to life. I hope our daughter one day finds a partner who believes in and supports her as her father has so consistently done for me.

I hope all of these people feel proud of this book and the effort to help more Canadians know the women who have led the way. This book would not exist without them. Any errors or omissions are mine alone.

INDEX

Cournoyea, Nellie: advice for women considering politics, 109; awards and honours, 99; on community involvement, 100–102, 106–107, 109; on elders, 100, 101; inspirational to women, 92–93, 99, 110; media career, 100–102, 103–104; as MLA, 104–107; personal history/family of, 98, 100–102; as premier of NWT, 98, *99*, 107; survivor of residential school, 98; on women's experience in politics, 107–109; work with land claims negotiations, 98, 103–105, 229
COVID pandemic, 85, 91, 93–94
Criminal Code, and women's rights, 16

D
Dalhousie University, 59
Davidson, Paul, 211–212
Divinsky, Nathan, 20, 26
Don Valley West, 202, 211–212
Duncan, Pat: advice for women considering politics, 119; early interest in politics, 114, 115; election campaign, 116–118, 229; as MLA, 111–112, *112*; on motherhood and politics, 115–116, 119; personal history/family of, 111–112, 114, 115–116, 119, 229; as premier of YT, 111–112, *113*, 117–119; sexism faced as premier, 116–117, 118–119; work at Chamber of Commerce, 114
Dunderdale, Kathy: advice for improving future, 139–140; on being a woman in politics, 126–128, 132, 135–136; career in municipal politics, 121, 126–128; early interest in politics, 121, 126; feminism of, 126; impact of politics on family, 137; lobbying against fish plant closing, 121, 124–125; love of community, 138–140; as MHA, 128–131; on NL and men's vs. women's roles, 138–140; personal history/family of, 121, 124, 126–127, 131–132; personality, 122; policies/

social agenda, 121, 124–125, 134; as premier of NL, 121–122, *123*, 131–137; run for party leadership, 133–135
Dunderdale, Peter, 127, 131–132, 137
Dylan, Bob, 204

E
École Polytechnique massacre (1989), 16
Edelman, Hope, 19
Edelman, Sue, 117
Edmonton, 111, 168, 170, 188, 194–195
Election Act of Canada (1890), 111

F
Facebook, 137
Fairview, 167, 170
Felder, Hershey, 35
feminism *see also* women in politics; women's rights; evolving dialectic, 198; feminists in politics, 33, 114, 126, 146–147, 205–207; and gender-based analysis, 176; resistance to gender stereotypes, 19, 207
First Nations *see* Indigenous peoples
Fishery Products International, 121, 124–125
fishing industry, in NL, 121, 124–125, 139
Flin Flon, 86
Fortin, Pierre, 164
French language rights, 145, 157–158

G
Ghiz, Joe, 61, 63–64
glass cliff, 31, 35, 76–77, 83, 148, 227
Globe and Mail (newspaper), 112, *113*, 118
Godfrey, John, 212
Gore, Al, 194
Graham, Kate: considering political career, 202; family history, 56; teaching career, 17
Green Party of Canada, 68, 81
gun control, 16, 33

157–158; assessing political career, 164–165; on being a woman in politics, 148–153, 160; career in social services, 141, 144–146; and CPE policy, 149–150, 164–165; early interest in politics, 144; early political career, 141–142; education, 141, 144–145, 151; election campaigns, 142, 152–153; on equality in home life, 146–147, 148–150; as leader of Official Opposition, 142; as leader of PQ, 150; on motherhood and politics, 148–150; pain of 2014 defeat, 159–160; personal history/family of, 141, 142, 144, 146–147; personality, 154–156; policies/social agenda, 144–146, 152–154, 159, 160, 164–165; post-political life, 161; as première ministre of QC, 141, 142, *143*, 152–155, 157–160; on women's experience in politics, 145, 153–157, 161–165; working-class upbringing, 141, 144

Matthews, Deb, 213, 216

McDonald, Mike, 72, 73

McDougall Centre (Edmonton), 191

McGuinty, Dalton, 211, 212, 214

McLaughlin, Audrey, 35

McMeekin, Ted, 209

media: and allegations against Redford, 194; damaging to families, 137, 184; focusing on women's appearance, 107, 152–153, 199; sexism in, 31, 83, 112, 117, 118, 154, 175, 225; social media, 137, 218, 225

Meech Lake Accord (1987), 28

Mercier, Noémi, 142

Merkel, Angela, 163

Métis peoples, 88

Metro Parent Network (Toronto), 201, 209

Metro Toronto, 201

misogyny *see also* patriarchy; women in politics; blaming women, 35–36, 37, 136, 155, 195; cognitive biases, 31, 75, 150; language and labels, 78, 83, 94,

218; stereotypes, 37, 77–79, 81, 151–152, 179, 226; women judged by appearance, 107, 152–153, 199, 220

Montréal, 141, 157–158

Morton, Ted, 191

motherhood *see also* women in politics; as barrier to entry, 50, 53, 64–65, 84, 119, 148–149, 181; childcare, 50, 53, 115, 136, 149, 164, 180, 181, 229; halting careers, 76, 116, 206–207; and political life, 76, 115–116, 119, 148–150, 172, 184, 193–195, 206–207, 226

Motherless Daughters (Edelman), 19

Mount Allison University, 55, 58–59

Mulroney, Brian: and Campbell, 26, 37; leadership win (1983), 115; Redford as advisor to, 183; unpopularity/resignation of, 16, 28–30, 32, 40

N

National Assembly of Québec, 142

National Youth Campaign (1993), 73

Nepveu, Gerard, 145

New Democratic Party (NDP): in AB, campaigns of, 167, 174–176, 178–179; in AB, policies of, 177–178; in BC, campaigns of, 71, 75; in BC, coalition with Green Party, 68, 81; in BC, policies of, 171–172

Newfoundland and Labrador (NL): Dunderdale as premier, 121–122, *123*, 131–137; fishing industry in, 121, 124–125, 139; men's and women's roles in, 138–140

No Second Chances project: closing event for, 17, 223–224; conclusions of, 85, 229–230; interview logistics, 97–99, 142, 167

Northwest Territories (NWT): Cochrane as premier, 85, *87*, 88, 92–95, 161n; consensus government in, 49–50, 91–92, 98, 106; Cournoyea as premier, 98, *99*, 107; separation from NU, 43, 104–105, 107

Notley, Grant, 167–168, 170–171, 174

Notley, Rachel: advice for improving future, 175–176, 181; advice for women considering politics, 180; assessing political career, 181; on being a woman in politics, 167, 175–177, 179; decision to run for premiership, 172–173; early interest in politics, 168, 170–172; education, 168; election campaign win, 167, 168, 173–176; as MLA, 167, 168, 172; on motherhood and politics, 172; personal history/family of, 167–168, 170–172, 174; policies/social agenda, 170–172, 177–178; on political environment for women, 181, 223–224, 228; as premier of AB, 168, *169*, 177–179; re-election campaign and loss, 167, 178–179, 223

Notley, Sarah, 167–168, 170

Nunavut (NU): Aariak as premier, 44, *45*, 48–52, 54, 132; consensus government in, 49–50; separation from NWT, 43, 104–105, 107; social issues in, 51–52

O

Obama, Barack, 135

October Crisis (1970), 145

Ontario (ON): Campbell as P.M., 15–16, 32–37, 40–41; and Hydro One privatization, 217–218; unpopularity of Mulroney's administration, 16, 28–30, 32, 40; Wynne as premier, 81, 201–202, 215, 216–218

Ontario Institute for Studies in Education, 201

Option Nationale, 162

Order of Canada, 44, 99

Order of the Northwest Territories, 99

Osgoode Hall Law School, 171

Outaouais, 145

P

Parizeau, Jacques, 147

Parti Québécois (PQ): Marois as party leader, 147–148; Marois as

première ministre, 141, 142, *143*, 152–155, 157–160

patriarchy *see also* misogyny; women in politics; "boys' club" in government, 156–157, 180, 195–196, 212–213; Canada as patriarchal society, 79–80, 83–84, 108, 127, 199; conservative political constitutions, 86–87, 197, 212–213, 230; leaders as older, white, male, affluent, 43, 53, 93, 197, 212–213, 230; periods of all male premiers, 53, 64, 121, 180; political rules made by men, 60, 64, 77–78, 90, 108, 223–224, 228; public disinterest in voting for women, 32, 36, 53, 60, 76; traditional gender roles, 88, 126–127, 150, 152–153, 206–207; and women's imposter syndrome, 83, 108, 152, 155–156, 163, 180, 222, 225

Payette, Lise, 147–148, 152–153

PEI Confederation Centennial (1973), 59

Penikett, Tony, 116

People for Education (Toronto), 209

Petal Prairie, 88

political analysis: gender-based analysis, 176; Strength, Weakness, Opportunity, and Threat (SWOT) analysis, 131

Port Alberni, 15

Porter, Allen, 138–139

Prentice, Jim, 174

Prince Edward Island (PEI), 55–56, 59, 61

Progressive Conservative Party of Canada (PC) *see also* Conservative Party of Canada; in AB, overwhelmingly voted in, 167, 170, 184; Campbell as prime minister, 16, 30–32, 40–41; in NL, Dunderdale as premier, 121–122; in ON, Mulroney's unpopularity/resignation, 16, 28–30, 32, 40

Pupatello, Sandra, 213

PHOTO CREDITS

ABOUT THE AUTHOR

KATE GRAHAM researches, writes, speaks, and teaches about politics in Canada. She holds a PhD in political science from the University of Western Ontario and teaches in the political science departments at Western and Huron University College. Kate is the creator and host of *No Second Chances* (NoSecondChances.ca), a Canada 2020 podcast about the rise and fall of women in Canada's most senior political roles—a project that inspired her own political pursuits and this book.

Kate lives with her partner, Jesse, and daughter, Flora, in London, Ontario.

THE FEMINIST HISTORY SOCIETY SERIES

The Feminist History Society is committed to creating a lasting record of the women's movement in Canada and Québec for the fifty years between 1960 and the year of the Society's founding, 2010. Feminism has a history that predates the 1960s and continues long after 2010.

The energy that women brought to their quest for equality in these decades is beyond dispute, and it is that energy that we capture in this series. Our movement is not over and new campaigns are upon us. But the FHS series presents an opportunity to take stock of the wide-ranging campaigns for equality that occurred in Canada between 1960 and 2010. There was much transformative social, economic, civil, political, and cultural change.

We maintain an open call for submissions (https://secondstorypress.ca/submissions/) across a full range of approaches to the period, including autobiographies, biographies, edited collections, pictorial histories, plays and novels. There will be many different authors as all individuals and organizations that were participants in the movement are encouraged to contribute. We make every effort to be inclusive of gender, race, class, geography, culture, dis/ability, language, sexual identity, and age.

Beth Atcheson, Constance Backhouse, Lorraine Greaves, Diana Majury, and Beth Symes form the working collective of the Feminist History Society. Margie Wolfe, Publisher, Second Story Feminist Press Inc. and her talented team of women, are presenting the Series.